The Toy Job

A Lifetime of Toys and Trains

Barry Potter

CONTENTS

INTRODUCTION

There was a time in my life when toys and trains were not an everyday and all consuming part of it. Until recently it had been many years since I had given much thought back to those days, and it was only in contemplating whether to attempt this book that I found myself lying in bed trying hard to recall them.

Instead of sheep, I was counting the jobs I'd had out there in 'the real world'. After getting to twelve, I must have dropped off to sleep slightly irritated, as for some reason I had always believed thirteen to be the right number. Whether I had forgotten one or not, however, is incidental. The real point is that, although I was happy and settled in my personal life throughout that period, my career had definitely taken a few twists and turns.

There are some people who even during their school days have a good idea of what they want to do in life, and can see their future career clearly mapped out. Even for those without such early aspirations, now that more school leavers are going on to university there is probably enough time and opportunity for most of them to be steered towards the jobs that suit them best. I was someone leaving school with no firm idea of what I wanted to do, other than to start work and earn some money.

Collecting for more than thirty years and going on to make a living out of what started as a hobby has never stopped being a pleasure for me. It began with the chance of my acquiring the trains I always wanted as a boy. Then, after discovering just how many other trains and toys were out there and the whole thing turning into more of an obsession, the world of toys and trains became something I wanted to be involved with full time.

This book is not an in-depth study of particular toys or trains; far from it. The occasional idea I have had of writing in that way has so far quickly fizzled out, after I have weighed up the amount of dedication and research needed to do things properly. Collectors turned authors such as Chris and Julie Graebe, Allen Levy, David Pressland, Michael Foster, Pierce Carlson, Pat Hammond, Jim Gamble and Mike and Sue Richardson have my respect for the work they have done, covering their subjects with authority and enthusiasm.

I had been vaguely considering writing something about toy collecting in general when, out of the blue and completely unrelated to that, Allen Levy wrote on a postcard to me 'What about your autobiography?' What about it indeed? My first thought was, would anyone be interested in reading it? After all, it was not as if I had just returned from sailing single-handedly around the world, or was even someone being paid a fortune every week for playing football. Messing about with toys and trains for thirty years would not be one of the more usual qualifications for such an undertaking.

Then I got to thinking that perhaps if I could combine a fairly light-hearted look at my life with the experiences I have had in the 'The Toy Job', and also include a few thoughts and comments along the way, it might be something worth doing.

The first section of the book outlines my early life and tells how I got into toys and trains in the first place. My experiences in the world of toy collecting and my perspective on it I have grouped into four sections, namely running toy collectors fairs, dealing in toys and trains, running auctions and collecting itself.

Although the text originates almost exclusively from my memory, with some assistance on dates and places from back numbers of the Collectors Gazette, there are some people whose help and support I must acknowledge.

Above all, I thank my wife Marie. Not only for encouraging me with the book, but more importantly, for supporting me along this toy and train journey that we have travelled together. Whether it is having trains all over the house, being up until midnight to finish off the floor plan for a fair, or the telephone ringing at all hours of the day – she has been through it all and has been there for me and with me every inch of the way.

I also thank my sons, Simon and Ellis for their support with the book and also for never once being selfish when it comes to sharing out the workload at the fairs. Whenever I am tempted to think how they could have greedily wanted to do everything themselves, I recall how they have been more than happy for me always to share in the delights of getting up at 3am on a winter's morning, driving 100 miles to a fair and setting up the tables. It is nice to think that they are so keen to include me in these things.

Thanks are due to Lester Harrison, for loaning me all the back copies he could find of Collectors Gazette, without really knowing why I wanted them. My thanks also go to Robert Wilson for proof reading the final text.

The one other person I must thank by name is Michael Foster, whose advice I was seeking when trying to find someone with an even fuller collection of Collectors Gazettes. "You can borrow mine," said Michael, casually informing me that he had the lot; every single issue as it turned out from number one in 1978 to the very latest. I had not imagined for a second that Michael would own such a library, although having thought about it since it should have been no surprise for, after all, he is perhaps the daddy (metaphorically speaking of course) of most researchers in the toy and train world.

The truth of the matter is that, over the past thirty years, I have been fortunate in making so many good friends and meeting a far greater number of pleasant and friendly people in this world of toy collecting than I might ever have done elsewhere. Every one of them has unwittingly helped me to write this book, and I thank them all for that.

Barry Potter

BEFORE THE TOYS TOOK OVER

1

Trains, bikes and Chuck Berry

The autumn of 1976 and an antique and collectors fair was in full swing. Marie and I were at the Queen's Hall in Leeds, having booked our first ever table at a fair of any kind. As it was a general collectors' one, we would have taken a few things along from home – maybe a couple of enamel signs, a vase or two, some crockery or anything we had no further use for. The main items to be sold though were Hornby Dublo trains – engines, wagons, buildings, track – just everything that was surplus. Our prices must have been cheap, as the minute we were set up the buyers were round and goods began to fly off the table. A couple of people remarked on how they had never seen us there before and of course, as we all know well enough now, there is nothing like a new face turning up to suggest there might be some bargains about.

This was our first experience of selling anything at a fair and I loved it. We had a great time and by the end of the day had taken £75. Even better, this was not just a printed salary figure on a bank statement like I had been used to – it was real money, pound notes. I really enjoyed being behind the table. Chatting to people about trains and selling the things I was interested in was fun, and I can remember thinking how much better it was than I imagined selling fruit and veg, clothes or any everyday commodity on a regular market stall might be. As very little remained unsold and we had nothing more we wanted rid of back at home, there was no point in booking for the next fair. Even so, I remember hoping it was something we might do again sometime.

For most boys in the 1950s, a new train set was a popular Christmas present and mine was no different, except that it was not new. It was late in 1956 when some trains had been advertised for sale, either in the local paper or just as likely on one of those handwritten cards you would see in shop windows. Maybe I had seen the advert and told my father, I cannot remember, all I know is that we went to look at them together. They were Triang. The 'Princess Elizabeth' locomotive and a tank engine, coaches, wagons, station buildings and a whole pile of the grey-based plastic track. This was not simply a train set in a box – it was a complete railway. My dad paid £10 for the trains on the understanding with me that they were to be packed away, not to be looked at until Christmas morning. I was ten years old.

Other than an Escalado horse racing game and some Dinky Toys, I cannot recall Christmas presents in detail before that particular year, although the one thing I do remember is the birthday card I received from my aunt the previous October. It was one of those showing your age in a big red number. Unfortunately, she must have lost track of exactly how old I was and on the morning of my tenth birthday presented me with a card displaying a huge number '9' on the front. Of course my aunt meant well and would not have thought it should matter too much, but as I was trying to be as grown up as possible and just getting my age into double figures, this did my image no good at all. For the next few days, whenever any visitors came round to the house, that card was kept well and truly out of sight.

We lived in Ripon, North Yorkshire, my mother's hometown and where she and my father had met and married during the war, when he was stationed nearby in the

Mum and Dad, with me in Ripon

Royal Air Force. My father (whose name, incidentally, was Harry) came from London and after the war in about 1950, he arranged for my grandmother (his mother) and my aunt to join him in making the move north to Ripon. Although not a blood relative, my Aunt Ivy, having lost her parents at an early age had been raised like a daughter by my grandmother. Living in London during the war, they both had vivid memories of the bombing and would tell me many times about the V2 rockets coming over and the nights they slept in Underground Stations sheltering from the Blitz.

Even without all the pandemonium of war, in those days coming to live in a Yorkshire market town after London must have been something of a culture shock. Although my father and even my grandmother never seemed to have too much trouble, my aunt would forever struggle with some of the northern ways and would often confuse Yorkshire people's natural friendliness with being a bit nosy. It was probably the Yorkshire accent, however, that she found most difficult. "People up here don't speak the Queen's English" as she used to put it.

An only child until I was fourteen, my childhood was a very happy one. Both my parents had been only children. This, together with my dad losing his father in the First World War and my mother losing hers some years before I came along, meant our family was not a big one. I had always known, more perhaps from my aunt than anyone else, the story of my dad's father being killed by a German sniper on one of the very last days of the Great War. Nevertheless, it was only after my dad died in 1990 and I got to thinking much more of him being only two years old in 1918 and growing up without his father, that it began to upset me. It was typical of his unselfish way that I could not remember him ever speaking about it, which was no doubt the reason I hadn't given it enough thought myself until then. Of course, as ever, the nicer the person the more unfair these things always seem to be.

My father had a fairly reserved nature, and was the sort of person who would just get on with whatever needed doing, without getting into a flap or making too much of a fuss. His placid manner in fact suited his job perfectly. He worked as a nurse in an old people's home. It is funny, but if you had a lady whose job was one more usually associated with a man, say a driver or a plumber, you would expect her to be known as exactly that, you wouldn't think of referring to her as a female driver or a female plumber. My father though was never known simply as a nurse, he was always spoken of as a male nurse. Even at school, whenever I was asked what my father did, I would always say he was a male nurse.

Where my father was very much a practical man who enjoyed doing jobs around the house or on the car, my mother had much more of a romantic personality. I am not sure where that leaves me, for if you asked Marie she would probably say that I am neither practical nor romantic, but there we are. My mother liked music and films, especially anything from Hollywood and would know most of the stars' names. I was about four years old when she took me to see my first film, The Wizard of Oz.

Although she did not play herself, my mother's love of music was behind her desire for me to play the piano. She would have loved me to be a pianist, and when aged about ten I had quite a few lessons, which at first I enjoyed. Miss Ingleby was considered a good teacher, but it was the practising at home that I couldn't apply myself to. She insisted on her pupils spending forty minutes at the piano every day and I was simply too lazy to do it. As I dare not admit that to her, I would invariably fill in the weekly practice sheet to indicate the forty minutes daily stint had been done, regardless of how little time I had been playing. Of course, when next week's lesson came around, Miss Ingleby could tell right away that I hadn't been practising nearly enough. She would give me a telling off and I would always promise to try to do better next time. There was no real improvement, and it remains one of my regrets, for my mother's sake especially, that I didn't persevere more.

Things were not much better even years later, when at sixteen and more interested in Elvis Presley than anything to do with the piano, I spent about ten pounds on a guitar and the Bert Weedon 'Play in a Day' instruction book. Who was he kidding? I don't think 'Play in a Year' would have made much difference. I did manage to strum a couple of chords in a fashion, but that was about the extent of it. The vague hope my mother had of there being a musical career ahead of me was finally put to rest.

The day my sister Susan arrived was memorable, in more ways than one. Not only was there now an addition to the family after I had been my parents' only child for the past fourteen years, she was born on the very day the Russian cosmonaut Yuri Gagarin became the first man to travel into space. I used to imagine being sat in the chair on a quiz show and for the million pound question be asked what that particular date was, then answer straight off the bat "12th April 1961".

Susan is a lovely sister, who sadly suffered complications at birth and is mentally handicapped. She has a happy life filled with lots of activities, including hydrotherapy and even horse riding and just like my mother she loves music. She lives with extremely dedicated carers. In fact all the carers we have met through my sister over the years have been really devoted to their work, which is wonderful for her and very comforting for us. Whenever we call to see Susan, the kindness and thoughtful ways that some people have make us feel very humble.

After getting the trains for Christmas, I was hooked on model railways. The interest was shared with my dad and in a small spare bedroom maybe twelve feet by eight, we very soon had a layout built on baseboards around the walls. Through the Railway Modeller magazine, I discovered the King Charles Sports Centre in Leeds (later to become Beatties) and going there with my dad was always special. The shop was on two floors and the second-hand train department upstairs was the place for bargains.

All available pocket money, as well as any cash from birthdays or Christmas was now spent on building up the railway. I kept faith with the grey plastic Triang track, which although already outdated, was cheap to buy second-hand, and I built a double track layout with one line climbing up to a high level. With just a little envy, I used to look at adverts for the Wrenn flexible track on the back cover of the Railway Modeller, but it was too late and far too expensive to change.

The railway was fairly complex, with scenery made from flour paste and paper over wire supports and lichen to represent trees. Even the grey sides of the track were disguised by sticking on birdcage grit to look like ballast. It was one of those layouts where you crawled underneath to a centre section, to get to the controls. The whole thing filled the small bedroom and I was really proud of it. One day, when I was ill and confined to bed, the doctor had called to see me. The door to the train room was ajar and as he was leaving he must have noticed the train layout, and popped his head around to have a better look. Maybe I had deliberately left the door open a bit so he would see in, I am not sure, but I remember being really chuffed when he came back into my bedroom to ask me some questions about it.

Trips to Leeds and the King Charles Sports Centre were always the best, but even back in Ripon we had two shops where trains were sold. Very much the up-market one of these was Collinsons, who were not Triang but Meccano agents, which meant that they stocked the range of Hornby Dublo trains. Collinsons was a large, good quality toy and sports shop, with the front door recessed into a large walk-in vestibule area, providing extra window space. Hornby Dublo was always on show just to the left of the doorway, where the locomotives were set out on a number of close-mounted glass shelves one above the other, making an eye catching display.

Being used to the basic plastic Triang engines, these metal-bodied locomotives with their detailed valve gear seemed in another league altogether and definitely left an impression on me. I was only window shopping though. Even if I could have afforded them which I couldn't, it was just not possible to mix these 3-rail Hornby Dublo trains with my 2-rail system. I wasn't too bothered – I was having a lot of fun building up my Triang railway.

Ripon's other shop with only a few trains for sale was Jack Thompson's, a long- established cycle, model and toy shop in North Street. It was a place I had been aware of from an early age, as my grandmother's house where I was born and my parents' first house were both just

With my Dad, and our Austin A35

around the corner. Mr. Thompson, who had taken over the running of the shop following his father George's retirement, was a tall very serious looking gentleman, always dressed in one of those long brown overall type coats which were popular with some shopkeepers at the time. Cycles were his main line of business and he had them all lined up outside. The shop had a long history of selling cycles and Mr. Thompson even owned an ancient penny-farthing, which he used to take along to garden fêtes and suchlike to demonstrate his riding skills.

His shop was a large two storey probably Georgian property, with one or two big windows to the left of the front door and a smaller one to the right. The upstairs rooms must have been used for storage, as I am certain that no one ever lived there. Given that after the shop was demolished a small supermarket was built on the site, that might give an impression of its size. Although it was a big shop, in all the time I can remember I saw only Mr. Thompson working there, with never anyone to help. As there was so much to look after, if ever there were more than two or three kids around at the same time, his attention always seemed to be focused on making sure nothing was going missing. Probably with good reason, as one of my earliest memories is of a much older boy jumping onto one of the bikes parked outside the shop and riding off, with Mr. Thompson shouting loudly and chasing after him down the street.

The most notable feature of Jack Thompson's though, was the amount of stock inside the shop. Anyone coming through the door had to navigate a sort of twisting path through all the piles of boxes and stock (not unlike the houses of one or two collectors we know today perhaps), only just wide enough to get them through to the counter. Equally surprising was that amongst all this apparent chaos, he would always know where absolutely everything was kept. I would ask him for a particular Airfix kit or a couple of boxes of caps and he would disappear off into the back area for what seemed like ages, then suddenly appear with the very item.

His approach to window display was equally haphazard. Rarely bothering to take any old stock out of the window, he would simply balance the fresh items right on top. The one permanent fixture I remember was a group of plastic aeroplanes hanging in the right hand window, which although gathering dust, being suspended on strings saved them from being buried under a pile along with everything else.

Whilst Mr. Thompson's shop was a large one and full of general toys, model kits and cycle parts, the amount of Triang items he stocked was quite small and as any fresh deliveries were infrequent and irregular, I never paid too much attention to the trains he had. One day I had travelled with my dad to Leeds, only to end up disappointed to discover that a newly released Triang locomotive I wanted had not yet arrived in stock. After seeing nothing in the Harrogate shops either, we returned to Ripon. By this time Mr. Thompson's shop was closed, but peering through the window at his disorganised jumble of toys, novelties, kiddies fishing nets, plastic kits and dozens of cycle parts, I could see the very engine I was after, staring back at me as large as life.

Years later, probably when the shop was earmarked for demolition, Mr. Thompson moved to new premises further down North Street where he carried on trading until retirement. I can only think that he must have had a clear out of stock around the same time, for the new shop was much smaller and certainly more orderly.

It must have been around 1975, after I was married and we had moved away from Ripon, when my mother gave me a newspaper cutting reporting on an auction at Tennants in Leyburn of the remaining stock from Jack Thompson's. Accompanying the article was a photograph taken in the saleroom, showing none other than the dealer Tim Armitage seated on the front row. As it was unlikely that he had gone along to buy those plastic aeroplanes, it suggested there must have been something in the sale worth having. Years later Rod Ward from Leeds told me he too had been at the auction. I know it was one I missed for sure.

The model railway interest continued until I was about thirteen or fourteen, when, after getting a brand new Raleigh racing bike one Christmas, cycling became more important. The term 'racing bike' here might be a touch fanciful – it wasn't one of those ultra lightweight jobs you see with the fancy gears for serious riding. The gears were in fact good old standard Sturmey Archer, with a 3-position operating switch and a large chromed hub on the rear wheel, although with the drop down handlebars the bike did look the part.

There was also a rack for two plastic drink bottles clipped onto the front, which I can't remember ever using much. It was almost as though the rack and bottles were there to give you the feeling that despite the fact you were riding a normal bike with Sturmey Archer gears, on the very spur of the moment you could suddenly zoom off and join in the Tour de France. Anyway, with the bike I was mobile and, together with a couple of friends, having a great time.

The railway line through Ripon was a relatively minor one, running between Harrogate and Northallerton. It was only eleven miles by bike, however, to Thirsk, which was the nearest point from Ripon to the London to Edinburgh East Coast main line and a cracking place for train spotting. Thirsk station was fairly small. Slow lines used mainly by goods and a few stopping trains ran on the outside of two island platforms, leaving the fast tracks to flow straight as an arrow through the

My friend Robert (right) and me on our 'racing bikes'

middle. Being in the centre of a long straight section of main line meant that express trains would always roar through Thirsk at top speed. Nowadays, a large concrete and wire fence separates the platform edges from the fast lines, but back in 1959 there were no such safety considerations.

Standing on the platform looking north, you would first see a shimmer in the distance, then after maybe the full minute or more it took the train to reach the station edge, there would be no more than two seconds to make out the engine's number before it flew past. This was the line of the streamlined A4s or 'streaks' as we called them, and they were the engines we wanted to see most of all. These locomotives, which included the record breaking 'Mallard', were special, and seeing that distinctive shape hurtling towards you at full speed is something that forever sticks in the memory.

Occasionally, when there was maintenance work to do, or a problem with this stretch of main line, these express trains could even be diverted through Ripon. Leaving the main line near York, traffic would be routed along our local line to eventually re-join the tracks heading north at Northallerton. When this happened,

A4 'Mallard' approaching Thirsk in 1959

on rails where on any other day of the year only local trains were to be seen, all manner of top link expresses sometimes even with Pullman cars would be coming by, clattering over the Iron Bridge across the river and through the station.

Unlike Thirsk, where these trains would fly past at full pelt, speed limits on our local line were much lower and it was great to see these main line engines, including even the A4s, slowly trundling through. Nowadays, there is not a railway line of any sort running through Ripon. The station building itself still stands and has been put to another use, but the track has all been taken up and the Iron Bridge over the river has vanished completely. This they say is progress.

After leaving Ripon Grammar School, my first job was in the Civil Service as a clerk at the Post Office Savings department in Harrogate, which was a thirty-minute ride each way from home, at first on a number 36 bus and later by car with some work colleagues. I worked in what were known as 'the huts'– a local term used to describe a large group of ugly pre-fabricated buildings, surviving from before World War II days. Post Office Savings was a big employer in Harrogate and at the time I was one of more than a thousand staff working there. I met some nice people and made some friends, but the work itself was dire.

Looking back now, apart from a hazy memory of writing savings account details by hand onto large card ledgers, the only task connected with work I clearly remember doing there is completing the forms to start my pension. Pension? – I was sixteen years old. No matter; this was the Civil Service. These things were carried out according to the rules and I had to know about my pension rights.

Years later, I believe to coincide with the manual records being transferred onto computers, the whole Post Office Savings department was moved from Harrogate to Glasgow. The huts were demolished and a large housing estate now stands on the site.

By the time I started working, a good few years had passed since the model railway had been used and there seemed no point in hanging onto it. The old Triang track was not wanted, but I packed up the locomotives and rolling stock and posted the whole lot down to the Southgate Hobbyshop. The £10 they sent me in return was the same amount my dad had spent on the trains to start with. Nevertheless, I had definite plans for the money. That tenner was the deposit on a second-hand, but very clean Capri scooter.

The motorcycle dealer in Ripon actually had two Capri scooters for sale, and as my best friend David Bairstow also fancied a set of wheels, I bought one and he reserved the other. I already had my provisional driving licence, unlike Dave who had only just applied for his, so the scooter with his name on had to remain at the dealers until it came through. I was all ready to go and he was grounded, as a learner's licence did not permit the carrying of a pillion passenger. As we used to go everywhere together, all this became very frustrating. He was still waiting for his licence and as I reckoned I was getting pretty competent at riding the scooter, one evening we decided to risk it. I took off the 'L' plates, Dave jumped on behind me and we set off intending to ride the eleven miles to Harrogate and back.

I had previously been having trouble with the scooter's exhaust pipe coming loose at the point where it went into the engine block, but I had managed to tighten it up and was pretty sure it was fixed. We set out from Ripon and for about five miles or so we were going along like a house on fire. Then, just as I eased off the accelerator to go downhill, the bike began to make a heck of a racket – the exhaust pipe had become disconnected again. With traffic all around, it was impossible to stop there and then, although at the bottom of the hill the road swung left into a wide straight section where we could pull over. The very moment I glanced in the rear view mirror before stopping – the dreaded blue light appeared. As the police car pulled in front, although fearing the worst, I thought just maybe he might be concerned about the exhaust noise and nothing else.

Wishful thinking that was. The first thing the policeman asked was to see my licence. It seems daft looking back now, but I remember hoping that he might not notice it was only a provisional – even more wishful thinking. Next, he wanted to know whether Dave had a licence, to which he answered no, but mentioned that one had been applied for. My friend then bravely tried to deflect some of the blame from me, by claiming that the whole escapade had been just as much his fault as it had mine.

The officer cautioned us and was making notes as I told him that we were really sorry, it was stupid, it was the first time we had done anything like this and would definitely be the last, which was no less than the truth. Our pleading managed to cut no ice whatsoever with the officer, who warned us that there could be a prosecution. The evening ended with my tightening up the exhaust well enough to ride home and Dave being driven back to his house in the police car. Our parents were furious and all we could do then was to wait and hope that we might escape with just a warning.

The official court summons arrived. In fact there was not just one, but three for me and one for Dave and we were requested to appear at Ripon Magistrates Court. The same police officer was in court to describe the incident and we were there to plead guilty, admit the charges and just apologise the best we could. The whole case probably lasted about ten minutes from start to finish. Not much longer in fact than it took to read out the charges.

I was fined £5 for carrying an unauthorised passenger on the back of a motorcycle without a full licence, £2 for the failure to display 'L' plates, £2 for having a defective exhaust system and my licence was endorsed three times. In court, the officer quoted my friend Dave as saying that the whole incident had been just as much his fault as it had mine and as a result, he was fined £5 for 'aiding and abetting'. Dave still had not received his licence even by that time, but that did not stop the magistrate telling him when it did arrive, to send it straight to the court for endorsement. When you think about it, a few more 'aiding and abetting' incidents such as he had with endorsements to match and you could end up being banned from driving, before even getting your hands on a licence.

This, I am relieved to say, to date, has been my one and only appearance in court as a defendant. Ripon Magistrates Court, which has been used occasionally in the TV series Heartbeat is now a museum, as is the old jail house – but at least I never appeared there.

As soon as Dave had his licence and scooter, we were out and about all over the place. This included a week's holiday with another friend Tony. The three of us travelled to Butlins Holiday camp near Filey, not far from Scarborough. I think we were all seventeen. I know for sure we were not officially old enough to be served in licensed premises, but we were away from home and no one seemed too worried about that. Anyway, I remember us walking, with probably the same sort of swagger John Wayne used to have in the cowboy films, into a very large bar, where in the middle of the room stood a revolving mini bar for serving cocktails. Completely circular and all crystal, lights and mirrors, it looked a bit like a sort of fairground ride for adults and was something we just had to try out. We stepped onto it and perched ourselves on bar stools, whilst the whole thing continued to move slowly round. There was a lady in the centre serving the drinks, and we were sat there trying our best to look like three sophisticated men of the world.

We had probably never even tasted spirits before, but when the lady asked us what we would care to drink, Dave ordered something like vodka and orange and I maybe a whisky and dry ginger, as though it was something we did every day. When she came to Tony, he said "I'll have a pint of bitter please" to which the lady replied "I'm sorry sir, this is a cocktail bar, we don't serve pints". This probably threw Tony a bit and his considered response was "I'll have a half then please." I don't remember what he finished up with. All I do know is that after drinking up and then slinking away in embarrassment, it was the one and only time we ever sat on that revolving cocktail bar.

Dave and I were both keen on rock and roll music, and on the scooters we would go to places like the Alhambra theatre in Bradford, or the Odeon in Leeds to see singers such as Little Richard, Roy Orbison, Del Shannon or Dion. It was the Odeon that we had travelled to in 1964 to see one of our favourite artists, Chuck Berry on his very first concert tour of Britain, when the supporting act advertised in the programme, The Swinging Blue Jeans (a proper sixties name) didn't appear.

With Tony and Dave at Butlins

We must have arrived early, as there were only a handful of us in the theatre, when the group that had been brought in as a replacement walked in from behind where we were sitting. They were fooling around as they ambled down the aisle, past us and off into a door to the left of the stage. They were The Beatles and as they were not billed to appear, I can only imagine that they must have particularly wanted to perform on the Chuck Berry show. True to form, when they finally came out on stage they were great.

For us though, and the rest of the audience that had gone to see him, Chuck Berry with his songs like 'Maybellene', 'No particular place to go' and 'Roll over Beethoven' (one of his songs also recorded by The Beatles), was even better. Just like the line in his hit song 'Johnny B. Goode', he could 'play the guitar like ringing a bell'. Maybe he had been studying the Bert Weedon 'Play in a Day' guitar book – or maybe not. As he had begun singing professionally more than ten years before that night in Leeds, Chuck Berry is one performer who has certainly lasted the course. I last saw him nearly forty years later in 2003 in a nightclub in Northampton, when he was well into his seventies, still playing and singing his classic songs. It was none other than John Lennon who said "If you tried to give rock and roll another name, you might call it Chuck Berry". He was exactly right.

BEFORE THE TOYS TOOK OVER

2

Amazing machines

It was during 1964 and in Ripon that I first met my future wife. Coffee bars were the places to go in those days and The Underworld was the name of the one Marie was in with her friends and I with mine, before we got talking together. Although we both lived in Ripon and had jobs in Harrogate, we always travelled to work separately. Neither of us had our own transport (I had sold the scooter just before we met). Marie always took the bus to work with a couple of her friends, and I was one of five people who worked at the same place in Harrogate and travelled there together in the one car. The driver charged his four passengers, I seem to remember, seven shillings and sixpence (37.5p) for the five days of travel each week, which, as petrol was about five bob (25p) a gallon, worked out fine for him and much cheaper than the bus fare for us.

Marie worked in the office of a motor company, which was not too far from where I was working and we would meet up every lunch time on a large park area in Harrogate called The Stray. It doesn't sound overly romantic, but we used to sit on a park bench eating sandwiches. I can't remember what we did if it rained – probably got wet, but you never worry about such things when you are young and in love.

After a couple of years as a Post Office Savings clerk, I left to take a job at Fattorini's, a high class jewellers also in Harrogate. Other than looking for something more inspiring than the job I had been doing, which would not have been too difficult, I cannot recall now what first attracted me there. I know I liked the people who interviewed me and perhaps I thought that the work might be interesting and different. Fattorini was a name well known in the northern jewellery trade and the Harrogate shop was, and still is, the only one trading under it and still family owned after Antonio Fattorini founded the business in 1831.

After being stuck in a drab office with the dull monotony of the civil service job, working here with no more than seven or eight very nice people, including the owners of a well run family firm, gave me the feeling of being part of something that really mattered. We were selling top quality jewellery, silverware, clocks and watches and I really enjoyed it.

I always liked the formal, yet friendly way we treated customers and indeed other colleagues. As I am sure is still the case in many high-class shops even today, management and staff were always addressed by surname. At eighteen years of age, however, to be referred to as 'Mr. Potter' every time by the people I was working with every day, took a little getting used to.

Our customers were generally quite affluent, mainly local people, although I particularly recall the day an American strolled into the shop. After making a purchase, he asked for directions to another 'store' in the town. As I explained to him, where he was intending heading could not have been more than five hundred yards away at the most. He was walking out of the door, as I was instructing him to turn left here and right there. "Don't worry", he said "I'll grab a cab" and he was out and away before I could say any more. Stepping into Parliament Street, Harrogate was not exactly like Fifth Avenue, New York, where yellow cabs would be cruising up and down every second of the day. Things just did not work that way in nice genteel old-fashioned Harrogate, certainly not back in 1965 when I imagine you could walk around for an hour or more without ever seeing a taxi. He didn't return, so I guess, as our transatlantic cousins might say, he must have made it there somehow.

At the time, I was keen on the whole jewellery business and even took an examination at Goldsmith Hall in London, in due course acquiring my Retail Jeweller's Diploma. If my mother was still alive, I know she would tell me it is a good thing to keep by, just in case this toy and train nonsense ever finishes and I need to get a proper job again.

As much as I enjoyed the jewellery trade, in the end it was having to work every Saturday I finally got fed up with, especially when most people had every weekend off. We did close on Wednesdays and it was nice to have a day off in the week, but it was not the same as a weekend. It seems a little ironic to be talking about Saturday working being a problem, after finishing up years later spending one day out of most weekends either at a toy fair or an auction, but there we are. I suppose it all boils down to what we think of as work.

Finally departing Fattorini's, I joined the Midland Bank (now HSBC) as a Cashier at the Ripon branch. Another respectable job, as my mother would say, no travelling to Harrogate every day and most importantly, every weekend off. This was two or three years before the new decimal currency was to be introduced and the old half crowns were being recalled in preparation. Dealers were advertising to pay three or four times face value for silver coins before a certain date and, working on the counter, we would examine every one coming in. I don't recall finding too many to sell, but it was good fun looking nonetheless. We also handled the takings from Ripon race meetings, which was great because for midweek fixtures we could volunteer to stay late and count the contents of the cash boxes brought in after closing time. This meant 10 shillings (50p) per hour in overtime and free race tickets for a forthcoming Saturday race meeting.

While I was there, the Chief Cashier, who, in view of the impending introduction of decimal currency was fittingly named Mr. Metrick, was finally retiring after something like forty years service, most of which had been spent at the same Ripon branch. I remember asking him if there was anything else that he wished he had done in that time and he told me that although he had enjoyed his job, he had always fancied having a spell as a long distance lorry driver. I remember thinking that it was hard to imagine there might be a lorry driver out there somewhere, just before retirement, saying the one thing he would really liked to have done was to have a go at being a Bank Cashier, but you never know.

By this time I was married and Marie had left her job to give birth to our first son, Simon. Young and happily married, we had everything we wanted really, except for one thing. If it is true what they say about money being the root of all evil, then we must have been living the purest of lives. We rented a small perhaps one hundred year old terraced house. It was one where the front door opened into the living room, a kitchen at the back and two bedrooms upstairs.

The house seemed very sound and although the only heating came from a coal fire in the living room, being a mid-terraced property it was easy to keep warm. Unfortunately, the solid floor had a slight, but nevertheless noticeable slope from the front door all the way through to the back. This didn't cause us too much of a problem, except that whenever we brought Simon's pram into the living room, we always had to make sure the brake was on, otherwise he would have been away and down into the kitchen in no time.

Before we took the house, the owner had tried hard to sell it and must have spent a lot of money on decorating each room and had even installed a new fireplace. It was probably the sloping floor though that deterred any potential buyers, and after remaining unsold, the owner eventually decided to let it. As it was, Marie's father knew a friend of the owner who told us that the house might be coming available, and if so, the rent would probably be very reasonable. He was right. It cost us exactly £1 a week. This was made up of 15 shillings (75p) for rent and 5 shillings (25p) for rates. There was one drawback however. Just like the other houses in the row, the toilet was outside. To reach it, you walked the length of the garden path and through a small gate at the end.

Mr and Mrs Anderson, the lovely elderly couple next door, had, as Mrs Anderson delighted in reminding us every time we saw her, lived in the same house for forty years. She also told us about the old gentleman who had lived in our house for nearly as long, until the day he was found dead in front of the hearth, with his topcoat on. I don't really know what the topcoat had to do with it, but it was always included in the story. It was Mr Anderson though who would never leave us in any doubt as to where he was heading, when he strode down his garden path. Just before reaching the gate, in order to save time he would unbuckle his thick leather belt, whip it off his trousers and hang it around his shoulders. At that moment, we could never understand why his trousers did not fall straight down to his ankles, but they never did. Goodness knows what kept them up. Forty years experience I suppose.

It can be fun to revisit a place where you once lived, but in the case of our old terraced house, although the row itself is still there, our front door sadly is not. What was a block of maybe ten houses has now become five, and our house is just a part of the one next door. Where the front door used to be is now bricked up. All nicely done with matching old bricks to be sure, but a brick wall just the same.

Things were fine at the Midland Bank, but I didn't feel I had found the job that was going to suit me forever. For one thing, the only route to promotion was by passing examinations in such captivating subjects as accountancy, economics and I believe legal studies. However well I might or might not have done my job counted for nothing in terms of job advancement, without these examination passes. For a time I tried studying at home through correspondence courses. Much like playing the piano years earlier, however, and probably more so as my heart was just not in the work, I found it a struggle.

We were happy enough in Ripon, but living in a small market town meant that there was not going to be much choice if it came to my changing

Marie, Simon and me in Ripon

career. The more we thought about things, the more the idea of moving somewhere else was appealing, perhaps near to either Leeds or York where there would be more scope for work. I really had no definite idea of what I wanted to do, but I began to scrutinise the job columns in the local papers.

Rowntree's, the confectioners in York, were advertising for a trainee Sales Representative. The idea of having a company car and swanning around here, there and everywhere whilst most other people were sat behind a desk, struck me as an attractive proposition, so I applied and was asked to go along to York for an interview. Everything seemed to be going well enough I thought, until I was asked how many of the company's products could I name. This was definitely a question I had not reckoned on, but I racked my brain and started to slowly reel off all the names I could remember, one by one like 'Kit-Kat', 'Fruit Pastilles' and 'Smarties'. After naming two or three more I began to struggle a bit, but still felt I was on the right track, until the man sharply interrupted me to say "That one's Cadburys".

I came out of the interview thinking, what a daft question, how could my answers to that possibly have any bearing on whether or not I would be any good at selling? Later on though, I reflected that maybe I should have gone in better prepared. Either way, it turned out to be entirely academic, as a polite letter came to say that I had not got the job.

A friend of ours at the time was loosely involved with computers, and he was convinced that they were the future and definitely the business to be in. The thought of getting a job of some sort in this modern technology seemed different and a little intriguing and prompted me to look at the job ads with more purpose. Eventually, I noticed that John Colliers the clothing company in Leeds were advertising for a Computer Operator. I applied and they asked me to go over to see them. The computer department was a new one in the company and the people I met at the interview were all young guys, who came across as really enthusiastic about what they were doing. The working atmosphere there seemed relaxed and yet go ahead and just the opposite of the traditional and very rigid ways at the Midland Bank. The whole thing seemed like a breath of fresh air to me, and when I was offered the job, I was more than pleased.

Accepting it meant that ultimately we would have to find somewhere to live within a reasonable travelling distance of Leeds. In the meantime, I needed to find a way of getting to work each day from Ripon. Whether I had dismissed the idea of travelling there by bus on the grounds of inconvenience, price or both, I cannot recall, but as I was familiar with two-wheeled transport, I decided to invest in a brand new Honda 50. It cost almost exactly £100 and was really something of a cross between a motor bike and a scooter. In truth, it probably had more the appearance of a moped without the pedals, although vanity would definitely have prevented me from referring to it in such a way. Economical though, it certainly was. Pulling up to the pump, I used to lift up the seat to get to the fuel tank and fill right up with half a gallon. It was impossible to get much more in, but that half a gallon would last for ages.

As the computer had to be kept running twenty-four hours a day, the new job entailed working in three teams on a shift system. The nice thing was, as a group we could decide among ourselves what our shift times would be. In order to have as much time off during two weeks out of three, we elected to work the first week from 7am until 12 noon and the second week from 12 noon until 6pm, which meant that the third week's shift would run from 6pm until 7am next morning.

It was great to have two weeks of very short hours, and starting at 7am and finishing at midday was like working a week of half days. The only problem came during the third week, when having to ride the twenty-six miles back to Ripon immediately after a thirteen-hour night shift could be more than a little tiring. On one occasion

riding home, I must have dozed off because I finished up in the verge, with the bike on its side and the engine still running. I wasn't hurt, but it made me think that I didn't want to be doing that sort of thing forever.

It was travelling to Leeds though, rather than coming back, that I had my most unforgettable moment on the Honda. Harewood Bank was not a dramatically steep hill, but it was a very long drag and more than a test for the 50cc engine in the Honda. It was very early in the morning and I was struggling up Harewood as usual, flat out at fifteen or maybe even eighteen miles an hour, when I could hear a car engine gradually getting louder as it was coming up behind.

Slowly but surely, I could see this blue vehicle coming past, when I suddenly realised what it was – a 3-wheeled invalid car. Embarrassment did not come close – it was the ultimate humiliation. Instinctively, I tried to pretend there was something wrong with the bike and even started tapping the gear change as though it was faulty, as if this was the reason I was just crawling along. Looking back, I am not sure exactly whom I was hoping to fool, as other than the invalid car driver and me, there was absolutely no one else around.

Every day after that, just before starting the climb up Harewood I was always careful to check in the rear view mirror, just in case the same car was sneaking up behind. I couldn't take any chances. Come to think of it, whatever happened to all those blue invalid cars, you never seem to see them nowadays? I don't know why not – they could shoot up Harewood Bank like nobody's business.

Renting the small house in Ripon had allowed us to save enough for a deposit on a house, and borrowing my dad's car at weekends, we spent a lot of time looking at the areas around Leeds. As it had always been our nearest big city and the place we would go to visit the large department stores, we were familiar enough with the centre, but the surrounding areas where we needed to look for a house were completely unknown. It was clear that living anywhere near Leeds was going to be quite different from the small market town we were used to. Nevertheless, we were probably more than a little naïve when it came to certain things, such as the wider meaning of the word 'village'. In our minds we merely assumed that any community described as such, would by definition mean something peaceful, pleasant and certainly rural, just like the picturesque places we were used to around Ripon.

I am really not sure what it was we expected to find, going to look at a property south of the city in an area the estate agent described as a 'mining village', but the slag heaps nearby were certainly not part of it. It was very much a learning experience. Eventually, after a fair amount of house viewing we came across a semi-detached property in Horsforth, a pleasant town just five miles north west of Leeds centre. We bought the house from the man whose parents had lived there since it was new in 1929. It had been well looked after with some nice original features like stained glass windows and was in a quiet road facing woodland. It was July 1970 when we moved to Horsforth.

Later that same year, we bought our first car, a dark blue Ford Anglia. It came from Frank, a friend I worked with, who sold us the vehicle after he had crashed it into our front gatepost. Coming to see us one day, he had misjudged the angle into our driveway and badly dented the front wing. He felt more sorry about our iron gatepost, but it wasn't damaged that much; the car had come off far worse. After a while, he came to the conclusion that he really could not do with the bother of having the car fixed and offered to sell us the Anglia for £65.

We had managed this far without ever owning a car and there were no immediate plans, or indeed money, to buy one, but this was too good an opportunity to miss. Frank, being single and with cash to spare, was probably yearning for something a

0-10-20-30-40-50-60-70 · · ·

a new shape jet-sleek from headlight to tail, a new spacious sense in light car design, a
new flexible, thrusting power performance, and British throughout! It's a dream of a car
that you'll learn to love for the thrill of sheer pleasure, broad grin of delight, and the
brand new idea of what driving pride it brings you. It's driving as never before, at
the wheel of the world's most exciting light car! In you get . . . key start, into first, second.
Crisp change, third gear at near sixty and snap into top. And away . . . exciting!

bit fancier anyway, so he was more than happy with the deal. A Ford Anglia, especially one with a bashed in front wing, would not have been the first choice of wheels for a young guy trying to impress the girls.

For us it was great – our first car. I had passed my driving test some years earlier and up until that time we had managed to borrow my dad's Austin A40 for an occasional day out. As he had never been too enthusiastic about this arrangement, especially since the day we had driven back from Scarborough without noticing a warning light coming on and so ruined the crankshaft, he too was pleased we finally had our own transport. Eventually I managed to straighten out most of the wing, and with a little filler and Ford blue paint to finish, it looked fine. It was the Anglia we were in, when trains re-entered my life the following spring.

"I'm not too bothered. You go and have a look if you like," I said, "I'll wait here." This was a Sunday afternoon in April or May 1971 and we were making our way home from a day out with our two boys – Simon, and Ellis, who was then only a few months old. We were driving through Addingham near Ilkley, when Marie

the all-new FORD ANGLIA

spotted a farmhouse chair standing on the pavement outside an antiques shop. She had a fancy at the time for a 'Windsor' style chair for the kitchen. Anyway, I stopped the car, parked up and stayed with the boys, whilst Marie crossed over the road to the shop. She returned to report the Windsor chair was too expensive (they always were). Now, although she must have known something about the hobby I had as a boy, she certainly had no idea of what she was getting herself into when she said "There are some trains in the window. Why don't you go and have a look?"

It would be wrong to say it seems like yesterday, it feels more like it actually was – a long time ago, but I can remember it well enough. These were Hornby Dublo 3-rail trains. A 'Bristol Castle' and a 2-8-0 Goods locomotive, both with their original boxes, perhaps four or five coaches, a few wagons and a fair amount of the 3-rail track and points, transformer, controller and a price tag of £15 for the lot. Here at last was the chance to have the trains I never had as a boy, but looked at so many times in Collinsons shop window in Ripon. I went inside to see the man. He brought them out of the window and after a friendly discussion I paid him £12 and could not wait to get them home. Of course, as any self-respecting Hornby Dublo collector would expect, both engines worked perfectly first time.

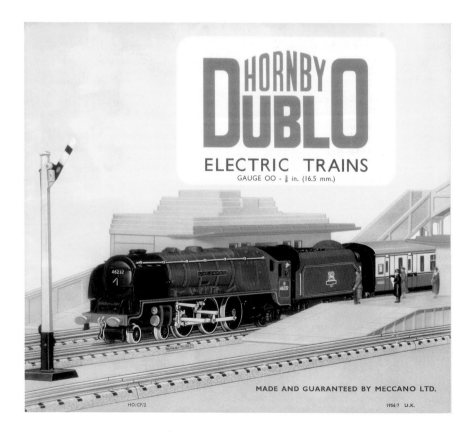

It was great to get my first trains in adult life, but it was not 'all systems go' as far as adding more was concerned. For one thing, with two young children and only one of us working, there was not much money to spare and even if there had been, where would I have found any more of this old stuff anyway? Progress on the train side was slow for quite a while. There were other priorities.

In the early 1970s, the computer industry in this country was really in its infancy and a completely different world from today, where computers are everywhere. Back then, it tended to be only the larger companies, or others whose management were determined to have this technology of the future at whatever cost, that were using computers. These companies would inevitably have a computer department, manned by a batch of newly recruited and always young specialist staff and a machine about the size of a small house. In many companies, the computer department tended to function in a completely stand alone fashion from the rest of the organisation and was sometimes even seen as a little alien to it.

Because it was something new and unfamiliar to them, established staff in other departments would more than likely view the whole computer set-up with a combination of mystery and suspicion. To these people used to the old ways of doing things, this new monster machine with its flashing lights, punched cards and reels of magnetic tape whirling around, often seemed more like something from 'Dr. Who' than anything remotely relevant to their business.

Occasionally, someone from another department would walk into the computer room either to deliver something, or perhaps just out of curiosity. With no end of lights flashing on and off and tapes spinning round, we could always tell from their bewildered expression that they were wondering what the devil was going on in this strange and mysterious place. Of course this would play right into our hands, and without making the machine actually do anything, we would start pressing buttons to make the lights flash even more, maybe feed some punched cards through and start talking in code as though we were handling some sort of secret mission. The person would then leave the room with an even more baffled look than before. We liked to believe that they would be going away thinking – 'Hey, those guys must be really amazing to know all that stuff', when in reality they probably thought we were round the twist. It was all good fun.

For me, the whole computer world has now been turned completely on its head. Thirty-five years ago when I was up to my neck in this brand new technology, the man in the street would have about as much understanding of computers as he would a probe to Mars. Nowadays, every single person you come across from six years of age upwards is an expert and I feel like bottom of the class. What with Jpegs, Gifs, acrobat, ebay, e-mail and the whole internet business, suddenly everyone you speak to seems to know simply everything there is to know about these amazing machines, and, as Manuel from Fawlty Towers would say, "I know nothing".

Companies were taking on computers for the first time, whilst others were expanding existing departments and there were good opportunities for experienced people all the while. I could have stayed on the operating side, as some jobs there were fairly well paid, but ultimately I wanted to be a Systems Analyst. I am really not sure whether it was the appeal of the job itself or more that I thought the job title sounded good, but that is what I wanted to do. The only problem was, in order to get there, I first had to understand something about computer programming.

With all the jobs on offer in the computer industry at the time, and as I quite enjoyed going for interviews, I applied for quite a few of them. In the seven years we lived in Horsforth, I worked for six different companies. After John Colliers, I joined Marston Radiators who had recently installed a Honeywell computer, similar to, but much smaller than the one I had worked on. I also managed to do some basic programming here, before joining Leeds City Council a year or so later as a supposedly fully fledged Computer Programmer.

As things turned out, it was fortunate that the computer department at the Council was a big one. It meant that my own mediocre performance could be disguised somewhat within the team's work, because it was here that I quickly came to realise my shortcomings as a programmer. I could see what it was we were trying to achieve in the task overall, but the technical aspects of writing the program I was unable to master. My programs would get the job done in a round about way, but they were far from being the most efficient. For a long time after I left there, I imagined someone finding a bug in one of my programs, looking into it and then collapsing in a fit of laughter at the way the whole thing was written.

After a year or so working for Leeds City Council, I joined the Provident Clothing and Supply Company in Bradford. Provident was an old established company with long experience in personal finance, based on agents operating from branch offices collecting weekly payments from customers' homes. Later, when I got to spend time at a couple of the branch offices with the agents or 'tallymen' as they were known, it was an eye opener for me to discover how so many people would buy almost anything on the 'weekly'. It was a complete way of life. Even things such as groceries, television licences and Easter eggs were not immune. Travelling around with the agents, I saw many houses the outside of which could only be described as grim, but as soon as you walked through the door you were entering another world.

Brand new carpets everywhere, new furniture, brand new hi-fi, new television, washing machine and absolutely everything bought on tick.

I remember one lady customer we had called to see who had found an error in one of her collecting books. Her entire family were Provident clients and at a time when £50 a week might have been a good wage, she was imploring the agent to get the error sorted out, because "There's forty quid going out of this house to you lot every Friday". Everything was geared to the weekly payments. Whenever a customer was looking to buy something from the agent's catalogue, the actual price of the item was neither mentioned by the agent nor asked by the customer – just "How much a week?"

My official job title within the computer department here was Quality Control Officer; a new position created following much inefficient and sloppy programming which had gone on in the past. They wanted someone to oversee the programming side and endeavour to make things more efficient, which, considering my experiences at Leeds City Council, was more than a little ironic.

Never mind the work, the most important thing I learned at Provident was how to play bridge. We had a regular lunch time session and I could not get enough of it. There was a young chap here who had only recently joined the company and he was one of those people who lived in his own completely make-believe world. To listen to him, there was just nothing in life he was not the best at. Whatever anyone else spoke about, he would always have to top the story with a tale of complete and utter fantasy. He wasn't part of our card school, but one day after he had been stood watching, he could not resist telling us about the time he had played bridge somewhere, picked up his cards and found he had four aces, four kings, four queens and a jack. Of course he just said "Seven no trumps", laid down his hand and made his contract.

As the chance of this happening, give or take a million or two, would be about a hundred million to one, we thought we might have a bit of fun. Just before inviting him to join our game, we set up the cards in the pack so that he would be dealt four aces, four kings, four queens and the ten of diamonds and, in turn, I would receive the jack. He picked up his cards, sorted them in order and said "You're not going to believe this guys – Seven No Trumps". I immediately said "Double". He didn't respond to that, but merely laid down his cards to claim his contract. After I told him that he was not going to make it because I would beat his ten with my jack, he criticised me for being very lucky. I just told him I had a sneaky feeling that the jack might come in handy. I don't know whether he ever found out what had really gone on that day, but at least it gave him another great bridge hand to talk about somewhere else.

As my bridge pals at Provident were Systems Analysts, it was really through them that I finally got the job I wanted. They arranged a meeting for me with their boss Alistair; we got on well and I managed a transfer to that section. Alistair was great. He was one of those people with the knack of being able to motivate you into always wanting to do the best job you could. Unfortunately, although all of us in his department liked him, I don't think he really felt a part of the established hierarchy there, which was a great shame and about six months later he was gone.

As far as the train side was concerned, although Simon and I did build a layout around the loft, things were developing only slowly whilst we lived in Horsforth. I hadn't come across too much Hornby Dublo in the model shops in Leeds, but then someone told me of a place in Bradford, called The Train Shop Supermarket. This was an unusual name for an establishment selling old trains – there were certainly no check out tills, or trolleys to wheel around. Even so, it was quite a shop and there were piles of Hornby Dublo for sale.

When I first visited there, it must have been well over a year since the decimal currency had been introduced and many of the prices in old money were simply crossed out and the new decimal amounts written alongside, suggesting perhaps that much of the stock was not shifting too quickly. There were piles and piles of tinplate Hornby Dublo coaches, all with ten shillings crossed out and now marked at 50p. Most things Hornby Dublo were available there and I would buy what I needed for the layout. I knew nothing of what was rare or hard to find, I just wanted a lot of trains.

It was outside the Train Shop Supermarket that I first met Jim Whittaker from Rochdale. He told me about his collection and made a point of mentioning his Hornby 'Princess Elizabeth' which he reckoned was now worth £55. As I listened to him, he struck me as a very nice man, but his talk of 'O gauge' was unfortunately lost on me. I had never really seen any and consequently had little interest in it. Jim would always refer to his collection as his museum and kindly invited me over to see it, which I did, although not until many years later.

When it came to family days out whilst we lived in Yorkshire, we spent a lot of time on the coast in the area around Whitby and Robin Hood's Bay. Marie's grand parents originated from Whitby and her family always had a special affection for that part of Yorkshire, and it was one we shared. The area west of Bradford around Hebden Bridge and Haworth was also a favourite of ours. For me, those reminders of the industrial past all around in the shape of old mill and factory buildings, and yet without the hardness you often find in the old coal mining areas south of Leeds, give the area a sort of rugged charm. We cannot change the fact that coal was mined in the south of the county and merely burned in mills in the west, but it has certainly left its mark.

We had more than a few family trips to Haworth and rides on the Worth Valley Railway from there to Keighley. At the end of one platform at Keighley was a small shop, perhaps it is still there, where I found a few Hornby Dublo items. Apart from model trains, the shop sold mainly real railway relics and second-hand books in aid of the Vintage Carriages Trust. I can remember perhaps the first time I visited the shop, looking vaguely at what must have been a complete run of 1920s and 1930s Meccano Magazines. They were tied up with string in bundles with a dozen (for a complete year), and priced at 75p a bundle. I had never seen any before, but I remember driving home thinking that they must be worth buying and as it happened we were going back there the following Saturday. Of course, whenever you see something for sale which looks good it never does to hesitate and, needless to say, when we called again they had all gone.

There is no doubt that in financial terms, I would have been much better off in this shop, paying attention to such things as station totems, signs and suchlike which have now shot up in value by leaps and bounds, but railwayana has never really been my thing. Even years later, when someone, who must have thought he had found 'the right man' as they say, called and offered to sell me two 'BARRY' Station totem signs for £65 each, I stupidly declined.

After a year or two at Provident, I left for a similar job at the head office of the Yorkshire Health Authority in Harrogate. The journey to work from Horsforth took a little longer, but the move was for more money and it was a nice drive to Harrogate anyway. By this time I had traded the Ford Anglia in against a two-year old Morris 1100. The £130 the dealer allowed me for the Anglia was exactly double the price I had paid and represented a decent profit on selling the car. I have since realised of course that selling any car at a profit is not the done thing at all. It just isn't cricket. So, after learning the error of my ways, I have always made sure it hasn't happened again.

Shortly after I started work in Harrogate, a very pleasant lad, freshly graduated from university joined our team as a trainee. Not having been to university myself, I suppose I had always harboured a little more respect for anyone who had. Unfortunately, it was whilst working here that my rose coloured perception of that wonderful world of further education and academic excellence suffered a bit of a setback. Whenever my new colleague stayed in the office for a sandwich lunch, his choice of reading matter was not The Times or even the Sun, or indeed any daily newspaper – he would always be sat at his desk completely engrossed in the Beano. Mind you, I dare say there is probably more to read in there than the Sun anyway.

Although the Health Authority head office was in Harrogate, I spent a lot of time in and around Halifax, on a trial project to computerise doctor and dentist patients' records. Before I had even set foot in the area, one of my colleagues suggested that if I get the chance, I should have lunch at the Halifax Infirmary. He was right, it was unbelievable. I understood in an instant why the health service took so much money to run. The medical staff clearly did not entertain any cut backs when it came to meal times, and rightly so. The food was good, the prices were low, and every helping was massive. I was on the Halifax project for about four months. The work was enjoyable, but lunches at the Halifax Infirmary were more memorable.

Early in 1976, I left to work for the Mintex Company, makers of brake linings and suchlike who were based in Cleckheaton, south of Leeds. The job was fine, but as things turned out this was to be my last one in Yorkshire.

Marie and I have always had an interest in old things (no reference to anyone's advancing years it should be said) and living in Horsforth, we would often call in at the Collectors Fair at the Queen's Hall in Leeds. There would be an odd purchase, maybe a kitchen stool (Windsor chairs were always too dear), a book or two, or one of those big ginger beer bottles which used to stand on shop counters. Among all the antique and bric-a-brac stalls were a couple of people selling toys and trains. One was Ian Clark, who sadly is no longer with us, looking after a table full of Dinky Toys and the other, Steve Sabey, an ex-policeman from Pontefract who was selling mainly Hornby Dublo trains.

Perhaps I bought the odd item from Steve, I am not sure, but as I was accumulating more Hornby Dublo than was needed, we thought it might be fun to book a table at the next fair ourselves. We did, and our first bash at selling at a fair was great. It was also a little too successful, for by the end of the day we had nothing much left to sell, so it was not an experience we could easily repeat. In fact as things transpired, it was the first and only time we were to sell anything at a fair whilst we lived in Yorkshire.

It was not long after this, and very early in 1977, that I replied to a job advertisement placed by Data Recognition, a manufacturer of optical document readers for computers, and based in Reading. They were looking for three or four people, including one located in the north of England, with computer experience and a desire to move into selling. Not since being turned down for the one in York years earlier had I applied for a sales job, but the idea appealed and I went down by train to Reading for interview.

I felt the meeting had gone fairly well and fancied the job, but even though there were no banana skin type questions about naming products such as I had come up against at Rowntree's, things were far from straightforward. Someone already with the company had taken up the northern area position. I was offered a job, but as it entailed looking after most of the Midlands area, if I decided to take it, we would definitely need to move south.

The thought of a complete break and a new start somewhere else was not unattractive to us. We had already moved seven years earlier to Horsforth and although our parents and my sister were living in Ripon, we had no real ties in the immediate vicinity of Leeds, other than schooling for the two boys. In the event, I think they too were a little excited about moving somewhere else anyway, so we decided to give it a whirl. As far as the job was concerned, I was required to stay in a hotel near to Reading where I was to be based for two months of training, after which time I would be working mainly from home. The dilemma though, was in deciding exactly where 'home' was going to be. We knew nothing of the Midlands area – north, south, east or west.

The one thing I did get with the new job was a company car. So after working in Reading during the week, at weekends, Marie, the two boys and I would just set off and drive around the Midlands in a gold Vauxhall Cavalier, looking at towns and areas in general. We dismissed the idea of Birmingham and anywhere in that West Midlands conurbation as being a vast unknown we would not easily relate to. Preferring a smaller town, we had a good look at Leamington Spa, for no better reason than we liked the sound of the name. In the end, we felt somewhere nearer to the M1 would be better, as this would allow us to drive up and see friends and family in Yorkshire more easily.

The two small Leicestershire towns Melton Mowbray and Market Harborough we took to, mainly I think, because they were market towns similar in size and feel to Ripon we knew so well. With a couple of specific areas now in mind, we began to scour the estate agents windows in earnest.

Expecting the task of house hunting to take much longer, we came across a detached corner house in Market Harborough we really liked, in surprisingly quick time. Dating from 1907, the house was in nice original condition and priced at not a whole lot more than we felt sure we could get for our semi-detached property in Horsforth. We moved to Market Harborough in July 1977 and this was where we were to live for fifteen years, before moving fourteen miles further south to our present home.

Looking back, it seems surprising that we found our first house in the Midlands area so quickly, as whilst we lived there, we were looking for another on and off for about eight years, before buying the one we have now. To be fair, looking for a house the second time around became more of a hobby than a desperate desire to move and we had a lot of fun checking out what was for sale and comparing different properties. If you don't need to move, then of course it is entirely different from the opposite, when you really do have to concentrate the mind. Although I might have flitted between jobs, it has not been the same way with houses.

Marie, Simon, and Ellis, shortly after we moved to Market Harborough

BEFORE THE TOYS TOOK OVER

3

Cut the price of toy collecting

In 1969, Tim Armitage ran what was probably the country's first ever swapmeet. Held in an appropriately named venue for a friendly gathering of like-minded people – the Fraternity Hall in Huddersfield – it boasted 44 stalls including one I believe for Simon Goodyear. Michael Foster's Ratley train fair in 1973 and the meetings of the Maidenhead Static Model Club also rank among the earliest swapmeets. The first MSMC swapmeet in fact took place on a Saturday in January 1971 at the Monkey Island hotel in Maidenhead. Whatever was going on in those far off days, all I know is that when we moved to the Midlands in 1977, the word swapmeet was completely foreign to me.

It was a world I knew nothing of, although one I would soon get into after visiting a Saturday swapmeet at the Ambulance Hall in Hinckley. It was not a huge building, yet it was crammed with tables and even more packed with buyers. I am sure it was here that I first met David Small and his son Richard, keen train collectors and good friends to this day. Others here included David Johnson, Paul Draycott and Keith Shakespeare, to whom I remember selling a mint and boxed Trix schools class 'Dover' locomotive for £18. The Hinckley meet was held every couple of months and it was great. The buying and selling was fast and furious and it did not take me long to realise that I was only one of many train fanatics out there.

It was at Hinckley where I met a collector from Coventry, and going back to his house gave me my first glimpse of a sizeable 0 gauge collection. He did not have a layout, he was more of an engine man and had most of them in original boxes. I am not sure whether it was more down to security or simply lack of space, but they were not kept where you might expect in display cases or even in cupboards. Some were stacked in the bottom of two large wardrobes and the rest were kept warm under his bed.

There was plenty of Hornby and the first large Bassett-Lowke, or 'Bassett-Luke' as he called them, locomotives I had seen. He took delight in showing me ones like 'Flying Scotsman', 'Princess Elizabeth' and 'Royal Scot' and looking back, there was something attractively mysterious about his pulling them out one by one from these unlikely places, as though he were showing me something forbidden. I thought it was slightly strange to see this very pleasant but unassuming man with all these nice trains, most of which I had never seen before and all kept tucked away out of sight. He refused to sell any of the 'Bassett-Lukes' unfortunately, but I did manage to buy a couple of Hornby engines from him.

It was also at Hinckley where I first heard people talk about Gloucester. "There's everything at Gloucester. Anything rare, you'll find it down there for sure," they would say. They were right. As I was soon to discover, the Gloucester Toy and Train Fair was definitely the place to be. Organised jointly by Trevor Morgan and Mike Rooum at the Leisure Centre on three Saturdays during the year, it was a magnet for everyone interested in collecting toys in general and trains in particular.

More than 200 tables were packed into the Gloucester Leisure Centre and on almost every one was a train I wanted to buy. It must have been here that I first came across such people as Vic Bailey, Ron Budd, John Martin, David Salisbury, David Pressland, Len Champion, John Cross, Chris Graebe, Lester Harrison, Bob Field, Mike Hobday, Terry Barnicoat, Irving Brim, Mike Brown, Roy Rowswell, Lester Saunders and many more too numerous to mention. Rare and interesting items were showing up all the while; it was great. The anticipation beforehand was a little bit like looking forward to a holiday or Christmas as a youngster and it was nice to experience those same sort of feelings in later life. I remember Mike Hobday telling me that he very often couldn't sleep the night before Gloucester.

Back then, any friends you had in the outside world (the one we all have to show our face in now and again) would sometimes expect you to be slightly embarrassed to admit to collecting toys or trains and were often quite surprised to find you were not. It is so different nowadays. With very changed attitudes and perceptions about collecting in general, people are much more likely now to simply accept it as something that others do, or even consider it a novel topic for discussion. Never really being one for participating in sports, or taking up hobbies like fishing or golf and certainly never having been at all curious as to how many pints I can put away in the pub every night, I remember when I first started going to places like Gloucester. I used to think that to go out and have so much fun messing about with the things I liked, just could not be right. Life was not supposed to be that good. But it was.

Not long after we had moved from Yorkshire, it was on a return visit there that I called in at a model railway exhibition in Harrogate and saw a working Hornby 0 gauge tinplate layout for the first time. Owned and operated by Peter Middleton, it was all very bright and colourful, with everything racing round at ninety miles an hour. Apart from the overall image of colour and shiny trains running on tinplate rails, what struck me most was the station named 'Ripon' and the clockwork 'Yorkshire' locomotive running around. In fact one of the first 0 gauge locomotives I bought was a 'Yorkshire', from a second-hand bookshop in Loughborough for £45. After getting that and seeing more 0 gauge at the fairs, collecting these bigger trains became more of a priority for me.

By the early summer of 1979, and after a couple more job changes, I ended up working for Wang Computers based at a branch office not too far from home. The address in fact would have been one more appropriate a year or two later – Railway Terrace in Rugby. I was selling computers and software packages to businesses, driving out and about all over the place and enjoying it.

One of my clients just happened to be in the model railway business – Slaters Plastikard the makers of wagon and other kits, based at Matlock Bath in Derbyshire. It was a Friday afternoon, their new computer system had just been installed and I had arranged to call in to see if everything was in order, before carrying on further north to see my parents in Ripon. I met with the boss, David White and after talking business for a while, he took me into the building that housed his wonderful 0 gauge fine scale layout, based on the Midland Railway. He ran the trains for a time and then we looked in at the sales shop he had alongside, where I spotted the latest edition of the Railway Modeller magazine and took a copy away with me.

It was only a brief visit to Ripon to see my parents and sister, although I did find time to glance through the ads in the magazine. Among the private 'For Sale' classifieds, was one listing a Precursor Tank locomotive and a whole batch of wagons in gauge 1, for which offers were invited. The ad sounded good, although oddly enough, here I was in Yorkshire and the telephone number was a Northampton one, only eighteen miles from home. The advert said to telephone after 10am, so I called the number that evening from Ripon, only for it to ring out without reply.

I arrived back home late that night and the next morning, ignoring the after 10am wording in the ad, called the Northampton number just after nine. The gentleman answering told me that he was selling the trains on behalf of his partner who was away on holiday, and that he had them with him at his gun shop in Northampton. I asked him what he meant by 'offers' in the ad and he told me that the price wanted was £550. I told him I was on my way.

On arrival, he ushered me through to a back room, where everything was immaculately laid out on a table and left me alone to examine the trains, whilst he manned the front shop. The Precursor Tank was clockwork by Märklin and in nice condition, although lacking a rear bogie. There were thirteen Carette for Bassett-Lowke wagons, all in virtually brand new condition and almost every one with its original box. At the time, I was just getting into 0 gauge Hornby and Bassett-Lowke and had never seen anything remotely like these before, but I felt sure they had to be good.

Amongst others, the wagons included a 'Colman's Mustard' van, 'Colman's Starch' van, yellow 'Bassett-Lowke' van, 'Trueform Boot Co.' van and three 'Bassett-Lowke' red open wagons. As I was going through them, the telephone rang at least three or four times before the man came back through to see me. He asked if I wanted the trains, as he was getting tired of the telephone ringing. There had even been someone offering to pay more money. I told him I would take them.

We packed everything into a couple of large boxes and brought them through to the front of the shop. I noticed on the counter a piece of paper listing all the wagons, which must have been written out for him by his partner. Checking the items against the list, I could see clearly written on the back 'Price for the lot £550. Accept anything over £450 for cash'. The telephone was still ringing away, so I just turned the paper back over and kept quiet. He thanked me for the deal, we shook hands and he handed me a £5 note to cover my petrol, which was very nice. I cannot recall

Two of the Carette for Bassett-Lowke private owner vans from Northampton

many things I have bought since which have given me more pleasure than those wagons, and definitely no other time when I have ever been given any money back for the petrol.

I began placing 'Wanted' adverts for toys and trains in magazines such as the Railway Modeller and the Exchange and Mart (whatever happened to that publication?) as well as local newspapers. The response was mixed; sometimes I would have nothing for a week and then the phone would ring with a couple of decent collections to follow up.

For a time, I even advertised in the local papers around Ripon and North Yorkshire in general. Taking the calls, I would arrange to visit whoever I needed to, during our next trip up to Yorkshire. In truth, I didn't have a tremendous response from the North Yorkshire ads (they don't like parting with too much up there), although I did have one call from a farmer. He had a Lehmann 'The Balky Mule' toy with the original box, which had belonged to his grandfather. After asking me to sit down at the kitchen table, he would not answer right away when I asked him the price, but insisted first on winding up the toy to prove it was in working order and we had it running back and forth. When I asked him the all-important question a second time, he simply said "I know these toys are worth money lad, and I'm not taking a penny less than five pund". It was the first German tin toy I ever bought and I still have it today.

Lehmann 'Balky Mule'
from North Yorkshire

Another reply to a wanted ad, this time from the Railway Modeller magazine, sent me on a memorable trip to buy Hornby 0 gauge trains. It would not be right to disclose the location, indeed I am not sure that I could find it again anyway, but taking a telephone call from a man and us agreeing a price for his trains, I drove out to see him. Armed with his surname and address, I managed to get to a village nearby, before driving around in circles looking for the particular house I wanted.

Eventually, I had to ask someone if they knew where this place was. "Oh yes, that is where Lord (whose surname I had) lives" and went on to give me detailed directions. From there, after finding and passing through a huge pair of iron gates, another mile or so further on and I was driving on a private road bridge over the motorway. A further half a mile or so and I could finally see the large house I was heading to. I rang the bell by a long chain pull at the door and the gentleman came himself to greet me, before showing me down to the cellar where the trains were kept.

The price we had agreed on the phone was quite high, but as he had assured me that the trains were in brand new condition, which was indeed confirmed as soon as I laid eyes on them, I judged it a decent buy. One of the locomotives was an electric No.2 Special LMS Tank and among quite a number of other items were two No.2 Special Pullman coaches and an electrically lit Goods Depot in its box. I paid the price agreed and we packed them up ready for taking away. He then asked if I might be interested in some other things he was not certain were any good and produced two very large circular biscuit tins, each packed tight with Britains soldiers. I had never been much interested in lead figures, but these, which were mostly helmeted British soldiers mounted on camels, looked to be good ones and he did not appear to value them too highly.

As I had already paid him a fairly hefty price for the trains, I figured that if the soldiers were cheap enough, I could do something with them. It was really a little tongue in cheek, therefore, that I offered him £20 for the lot. He hesitated, and for one terrible moment I feared I had offended a member of the nobility – at least we were not back in the old feudal days, when I could have been clapped in irons or put in the stocks for such an affront. Finally, he said, "If they are worth that much, I had better find out more about them". It was weird. The offer I thought low was obviously more than he was reckoning on, and instead of just wanting rid of them, he was now motivated to doing some research on the matter. I left the soldiers with him, but I remember driving home, wondering – not as might have been expected how high I should have gone – but just how low the offer would have needed to have been, to have bought them.

The Britains soldiers incident was slightly bizzare. Nevertheless, it can be difficult being in a position of having to make an offer for a collection, without having any clue from the seller as to what is expected. Probably the worst scenario is having to leave an offer, when you know someone else will be coming along later. It can be annoying to lose something you really want. On the other hand if you get the call to say "Come and pick it up, it's yours", the immediate suspicion might be that you have paid too much. If the collection is one you are desperate for and your offer is accepted, then of course that is great.

Occasionally though, after you have made an offer the seller might say, "Yes, oh thank you, I'm absolutely delighted – are you sure that's not too much?" After a response like that, let's be honest, we wouldn't be human if we didn't wish there might be an odd time when we could say "Look, let us start again. I'll begin at that figure and gradually reduce it, until your being ecstatic about the price changes to your being just nicely satisfied and that will be the price we will settle on". It is nice to see people happy, but in certain situations, maybe not deliriously so.

Travelling about with my job during the week gave me the chance to look in at the odd antiques or model shop, and on a visit to a company in Leeds, I called into Beatties Model Shop (formerly the King Charles Sports Centre). No second-hand train department there by that time – just stacks of new trains, kits and the like – except that in one corner there were two items which were a little different. Just like the gauge 1 wagons in Northampton, however, they were things I had not come across before.

One above the other on glass shelves were two Chad Valley toys, a 'Carr's Biscuits' double decker bus and a Dennis van advertising board games, and both in mint condition. As everything else in the shop was brand new, they must have been taken in as a part exchange. I had no idea what they were worth, but priced at £12 each, I knew I could not go far wrong. They were the first tinplate road vehicles I ever bought and from the very place I came to buy trains as a boy.

It was a fair drive from Market Harborough to Manchester, but we had booked a table at a toy fair in Sale on the first floor of the town hall, organised by Tom Spink. Before going, although I had decided to definitely keep the Chad Valley Games Van, the more I looked at the Carr's bus, the more it seemed plain if not a little ugly at the front. I concluded that it had to go and priced it at £30, hoping that selling the one toy would pay for the other. As soon as the bus was unwrapped and placed on the table, David Greaves, a man known more at the time for collecting Dinky Toys, had his hand firmly on it. He offered me £28 and I took his money.

That was the day I first met the journalist Jack Tempest. Jack was probably writing about collecting when many of us were still in short trousers, and his articles have appeared in no end of magazines over the years, such as The World's Fair and Old Glory, as well as the toy ones like Collectors Gazette and Model Collector. He has also written a book on toy collecting. A long time collector, Jack's interest has been mainly in novelty tin toys, although he did have a large collection of mint and boxed Dinky Toys at one time, which he enjoyed showing off at the fairs, including a trade box of six 'Oxo' vans in perfect condition. That day at Sale, Jack had not seen my

Chad Valley bus early enough to buy it, but wished he had and told me that in the condition it was in, it had to be worth £100 at least.

It struck me then, that this toy collecting business was an interesting game. 'Crazy' might be a more appropriate description than 'interesting' in my case, when you consider that I fairly recently paid more than seven times that price for exactly the same bus, admittedly with its original box. Something I learned about human nature from my selling days is that the first thing that nearly all of us do after buying something expensive is to 'sell' ourselves the rightness and wisdom of the decision to buy. Once we convince ourselves we were right to buy whatever it was, then everything is fine and we can relax. Perhaps that bus doesn't look quite so ugly after all, and, anyway, I know for a fact that *that* box has to be worth good money.

By the late 1970s, I was buying lots of trains and building up a sizeable collection. Wanted ads in the magazines were often fruitful and I would be out and about seeing people with items to sell. Sometimes it was possible to combine a buying trip with a visit to see a client on business nearby. On other occasions, I might arrange to see a collection and couple it with a family day out. Marie did not mind this happening the odd time, but if it became too frequent I wasn't always popular.

Chad Valley 'Carr's' double decker bus

Hornby 'Bramham Moor' locomotive

Just before setting off to see friends or family in Yorkshire, or heading for a day out in the country, she would enquire "Are there any calls to do?" – she knew me well enough. It was not a problem if I had already arranged to see someone about trains and then suggested that we might have a drive out there together. On the other hand, if it was the other way around and I had added a train call to a pre-arranged family day out, that was not always viewed so favourably.

I remember being at Marie's parents house in Ripon the day after Boxing Day one year, and announcing that there was a gentleman in Whitley Bay near Newcastle I wanted to see at sometime or other about trains. As it happened, Marie's dad fancied a trip out, so I called the man and after lunch, Marie, her dad and I enjoyed a pleasant drive up to the East Coast that afternoon. Amongst some other Hornby 0 gauge, I bought an electric 'Bramham Moor' locomotive with the box and in absolutely brand new condition, like it had just come out of the shop. We all had a nice day out and I drove back delighted.

All the time I was putting a collection of trains together, some items had to be sold in order to buy more. Having a sales table at fairs was great and together with Marie and often the two boys, I would be out most weekends at either a toy fair or a collecting event somewhere or other. The Tramway Museum at Crich in Derbyshire held an annual Transport Extravaganza over the three days of the August Bank Holiday weekend. Not unexpectedly, trams were the main attraction, but on an area of high ground above the tramlines, all manner of stalls were set out where transport relics and other items, including toys, were on sale. Regular traders in toys and trains there included Tim Armitage, Simon Goodyear, Roy Laycock, Colin Walker and Rod Ward.

Another Crich regular was Jim Varney. Jim was quite a character and someone who had been involved with toys for many years, even producing white metal kit models of road vehicles at one point. He was a large, bearded man and, with his huge Alsatian dog by his side, he looked like someone you definitely would not want to mess with. Under that tough exterior though, he was a nice man who thought the world of that dog. Driving all the way up to Crich from Bromley in Kent, he would always park his caravan in the same position each year and have his selling area under the same large tree. For fun he used to tie a few toys onto the branches, including at one time a car almost sawn in half with the hacksaw still sticking out, and a sign underneath saying 'Cut the Price of Toy Collecting'.

Anyone who has stood behind a table selling will know that, while for most of the time it can be fun, just occasionally someone will come along who could try the patience of Job. It then becomes merely a question of how tolerant you are, and unfortunately, tolerance was not one of Jim's best virtues. I remember well a customer looking for at least five minutes at a Dinky Toy in rough condition that Jim had priced at either three or four pounds. At least twice I heard the man say "It's a pity about the condition". Eventually, he put it down and walked away, only to return later and declare "Look, I can take this off your hands. I only want it for re-painting. What about a pound?" Jim picked up the car, carefully placed it on the floor and stamped on it. With the broken remains in his outstretched hand, he looked at the man and growled "Here – take it for nothing." He took it.

We had a sales pitch ourselves at Crich near to Jim's, and as well as toys, we usually brought some different items along we had collected, such as old enamel signs, old bottles and such like. It was a beautiful sunny Sunday morning one year and I was sat by the table, when a lady came up with some coins and, pointing at something, said "I'll have one please love". I looked across to see what had caught her eye and propped up against the table was a pre-war blue enamel sign with the large lettering 'News of the World on Sale Here'. I had to tell her we had sold out.

Gloucester and Windsor were the main toy fairs, but others were springing up in places like Leeds, Wimbledon, Manchester and even an odd one in the North Yorkshire town of Thirsk where I did my train spotting as a boy. Another general collectors fair we liked was the huge Bolton fleamarket run by Alan Whitehead, which was held in two large adjoining halls, one of which was full of motorbikes and autojumble. Everything under the sun was for sale there, and just as enjoyable as having a table was the thrill of looking around to buy. As well as the weekend fairs, there were also a couple of evening events we enjoyed. One was Mike Ennis's fair in Cuffley near London and the other was held in the West Park Cricket Pavilion at Lambley near Nottingham, organised by Dave Jowett and Colin Lee.

Although there can have been no more than thirty or forty tables at the Lambley swapmeet, there were always plenty of decent items to buy and the selling could be good. Tim Armitage (who else?) and Peter and Joan Dunk were among the regulars. One particular friend of mine, who had recently arrived on the scene, was especially keen on Hornby Dublo. He was prepared to pay top money for the best mint and boxed examples and would advertise the fact every month in the Wanted column of the Railway Modeller. He would place an ad, quoting prices he would pay for various items. We were good friends, but I did wonder when he was out buying trains from someone and desperate to assure the person that the deal was a fair one, whether just occasionally his surname might raise an eyebrow or two. His name was Dennis Cheetham.

Dennis was a big man and, just like Jim Varney, not the type who would tolerate nonsense from anyone, as a man visiting the Lambley Swapmeet one Thursday evening was to discover. Behind his table of Hornby Dublo as usual and with the fair going along in full swing, Dennis spotted a man pinching one of his trains. All of a sudden there was this really loud shouting which silenced the whole room, and everyone looked over to see Dennis take one massive leap right over his table into the aisle and wrestle the man to the floor. Dennis managed to prise his engine back and with some assistance kept hold of the culprit until the police could be summoned. When they arrived, after a brief discussion with Dennis and one or two witnesses, they proceeded to take the offender down to the Police Station for processing.

Just before he was bundled into the police car, he asked if he could use the lavatory. As soon as he re-emerged, the officers, obviously aware of every trick in the book, searched the toilet cubicle to find a small hoard of trains stuffed behind the cistern. The man had clearly snaffled no end of items before even reaching Dennis's table, and was now trying desperately to get rid of the evidence. Although the court case took the usual lengthy time to go through, I understand that he was eventually convicted. Apart from the entertainment it gave us, the best thing about the incident I felt, was that if there had been anyone else at the fair that evening with the idea of pinching even so much as a track clip, any such thoughts must have been snuffed out like a candle. I could not imagine too many being willing to risk the Dennis treatment.

As we both advertised for trains and saw each other at the fairs, I knew Dennis very well. Apart from being a strong no messing about type of character, he was also someone who enjoyed a laugh and a joke and it was he who figured in a telephone call I took one morning. The man on the end of the line began by telling me that he had seen my 'Wanted' ad in a magazine, and right away started to reel off a complete inventory of trains he supposedly had. He was reciting all manner of Hornby 0 gauge locomotives, such as 'Princess Elizabeth', 'Bramham Moor', 'County of Bedford', before going on into Trix, Bing, Märklin etc. When he got to the Hornby Dublo and started to tell me about all the boxed locomotives including Canadian Pacifics and no less than six boxed LNER articulated coach sets, I thought 'This is a complete wind up by Dennis Cheetham'.

Hornby Dublo appreciating by 20% yearly says Dennis Cheetham

From Collectors Gazette June/July 1979

"Come on Dennis! Stop messing about!" I said, "I know it's you." I paused briefly, awaiting a response, but none came immediately, and so I tried again. "Dennis. Come off it. Very funny, we've both had a laugh now." Down the phone I heard a sharp intake of breath, and the voice, with just a trace of annoyance, said "My name's not Dennis." And it wasn't. As soon as I realised the call really was genuine, I was full of apologies, telling the caller about my crazy friend who liked a practical joke and all the time trying hard to rescue the situation, which after a bit more talking I managed to do. Once we returned to the matter in hand, the man informed me that he had recently returned to live in Lancashire, after spending the greater part of his life in Canada. He had brought his train collection back with him to England, but as he was no longer so interested in collecting, he had now decided it was time to sell. I noted his name and address and arranged to travel up to Burnley in Lancashire to meet him and see the collection within the next few days.

Most of his trains, and there were certainly plenty of them, were set out in a very large loft room, where I spent an hour or so trying my best to take in what was on offer. The man had made it clear to me on the telephone that he didn't want to sell odd items here and there, so the whole lot had to go in one fell swoop and his price was £10,000. This was the late 1970s and frankly, I didn't have that sort of money, although I reckoned if need be, I could borrow it.

All the Hornby 0 gauge items he had mentioned on the phone were present and much more besides, including a rare post-war electric LMS boxed set and a boxed electrically lit Water Tower, a similar boxed Signal Gantry and Stations. There was a mass of Trix, some Bing in gauges 0 and 1, Elletren, Märklin and quite a few Bassett-Lowke locomotives. The Hornby Dublo was particularly impressive – dozens of locomotives including the Canadian Pacific models, and pile after pile of boxed rolling stock items. The six LNER articulated coach sets were present as promised, with the added bonus that they were all the rare post-war versions, complete with lift-off lid boxes and every one in perfect condition. The articulated sets I presumed, would have been items exported to and then sold in Canada.

Even now, I am at a loss to know why I did this, but after climbing down from the loft and him asking me how I felt about the collection, I told him that I was not exactly sure and that I would like to think it over. Looking back, it is plain that I had been nowhere near thorough enough in valuing what was there and, in my hasty appraisal, the £10,000 he wanted seemed plenty of money. The collection was worth a little more than he was asking I thought, but not really enough to justify my borrowing the money for. Anyway, I left without any deal being done, and this proved to be a big mistake.

Driving home, I was mulling over the things I had seen and trying to put more accurate values in my mind to various pieces. The more I thought about many of the rarer items, the clearer it became that I had underpriced far too much in that brief survey in the loft. By the time I had arrived home, not only was I convinced that £10,000 was a reasonable price, I felt sure that the collection had to be worth nearly double. I called the man immediately to tell him I would like to buy it.

The only problem was – he no longer wanted to sell. He had been talking things over with his wife after I had left and was very sorry, but he had changed his mind and decided to continue collecting for a while. Talk about regret. I didn't give up on it though and called him a few months later, eventually managing to buy about half of the 0 gauge and gauge 1 items. He still would not part with the Hornby Dublo trains, and after a year or two I lost touch with him altogether.

Although I was a fool not to buy that collection when I had the chance, after a while I consoled myself by looking upon it as a lesson to be learned for the future. In recent years I have seen two or three examples of those boxed post-war LNER articulated sets selling for around £1,800 or more apiece – maybe the same ones, you never know; it can be a small world sometimes. This means that at today's prices, those six sets alone would have been worth his asking price at that time for the whole collection, but that is the way things go.

Moving the clock forward twenty odd years to 2000 and the Rugby auction when we were selling the Markham Collection from Canada, an elderly gentleman walked up to me. "Barry, do you remember me? You came up to see me a long time ago." It was the very man whose collection I should have bought all those years earlier. Apparently, he had been a good friend of Al Markham's when they were collectors together in Canada. It was slightly surreal, but very nice to see him again after so long. He was a little frail by then and sadly has since passed away. He had no further interest in trains himself, for (as he told me) the rest of his collection had been disposed of many years earlier. Touchingly, he had made a special trip down to Rugby just to be there when his friend's collection was being sold, and sat on the front row all the way through the auction.

By the late 1970s, my lifestyle was becoming one of stark contrast, having a job in the week that was fairly intense, and then coming out at the weekend to a completely relaxed atmosphere at a toy fair. I was enjoying my job, but after coming home from a week filled with meetings, presentations and sales proposals and then going to places where people were just having a fun time, I was beginning to think seriously about what I wanted out of life.

There was no doubt that earning quite good money and having a company car would be a lot to give up. On the other hand, I was enjoying myself so much with these trains that, if there were some way of turning all this interest into a full time business, that was what I wanted to do. From having tables at the fairs as a collector just selling surplus items, the idea of buying and selling toys and trains for a living was appealing, although I was not at all sure, with a family to support that it would give us a reliable income. I felt I needed something more tangible. Marie was working in an Estate Agents office in the town and, helpful though her job was to us financially, she was working only part-time and her money would only go so far.

We had already started the toy collectors fair in Market Harborough, and the response to that convinced me that there would be a demand for more of the same in other places. Running enough fairs I felt would give us a reasonable living, and so, by 1980, I decided to take the plunge and leave my job to become an Organiser of Toy Collectors Fairs.

Ellis, Simon, and 'Flossie' with traction engines in Market Harborough

ALL THE FUN OF THE FAIR

4

A totally diabolical situation

Not so long ago I had sight of a flier for Michael Foster's train fair at Ratley in Oxfordshire, held on 1st December 1973, and one of England's earliest swapmeets. For an admission price of 10p, every visitor through the door was promised a boxed Hornby Dublo item as a free gift. Now even if you assume that the gift was not to be a rare Rail Cleaning Wagon, it still seems a heck of a bargain. In fact you cannot help but wonder whether anyone considered going out and coming back in again to accumulate the free goodies. I understand that before the day of the fair had dawned, costs had dictated an increase in the admission to 25p – maybe those Rail Cleaners were to be wheeled out after all? Whatever, it was just as well that Michael had finished his fairs before we came along, as I wouldn't have fancied competing with that sort of a deal.

5th September 1979, and a Wednesday evening in Market Harborough. This was the date of the first toy collectors fair we held at the Welland Park College and after 150 fairs in the same hall, the very last one took place on 23rd October 2005. Looking back, it is hard to know how long we expected it to last, but I don't think many would have put money on the 26 years it did.

It seems so long ago now, but we must have been fretting a bit before our first fair as we do even now with a new event. Market Harborough, however, took off right from the start. The doors opened at 7pm and by about eight it was difficult to move around the aisles.

Most of the well-known names in the toy and train world have spent time at Market Harborough over the years. In the early days it was people like Peter and Joan Dunk, Andrew Clark and Roy Laycock who came, while in later times others such as Bob and Sue Jones, Brian and Ann Holmes and Graham de Chastelain would take their place. Early on, as well as Peter and Joan Dunk, a few other dealers would come up from London including Jim Varney and Eric French, an actor who specialised in cameo roles and who could always be seen 'working at headquarters' in the opening sequence of the TV programme The Sweeney.

The late Peter Randall, joint founder of the Hornby Railway Collectors' Association and once a dealer in Hornby trains, was also a regular here. Peter traded under the name 'Binns Road' which, as all Hornby aficionados will know, was the address of the famous Meccano factory in Liverpool. A very nice man, Peter would always take the utmost pride in the appearance of his sales table. A lovely cloth was put on first and then all the stock would be set out very smartly, with not one wagon or even a coupling out of line.

At the back of his table stood a large wooden sign with his 'Binns Road' name in really big letters. One evening he had set everything up as usual and was walking around the hall chatting to the traders, when I drew his attention to the sign. The large wooden board came in two halves and Peter had set it up the wrong way round and it now read 'Road Binns'. Peter was mortified, this simply would not do. He didn't just walk back to his table, he literally ran down the aisle to put it right.

Many of the visitors and stallholders whom Marie and I first met there, are friends today – people like Phil Ward, Keith Hadley, Derek Robinson and Fred Kendall. Fred, who is now in his eighties, was telling me that, apart from the last two or three, he had attended every single fair at Market Harborough, either as a visitor or, as in the last few years with a sales table. Someone else told me that he never liked to miss this fair, because the bacon rolls were so good.

The London dealer Pete McAskie, as well as knowing a thing or two about toys, also has a theory about bacon rolls. The price charged, he maintains, is more often than not inversely proportional to the quality. In other words, the cheaper they are the better they are likely to be. This was certainly true at Market Harborough, where Mary and Peter Jacques, who looked after the catering, never charged too much for theirs.

Another regular trader at this and most of our early fairs was John Webb. Once John started running his own fairs, not only was he now in competition with us, but when he finished dealing we saw very little of him. I remember him buying a Dinky Toy 'Slumberland' Guy van from me at Market Harborough. He paid me £75 and it wasn't just a nice one, it was brand new in the box. Thinking about it, I am not sure if he understood that the deal was I could buy it back at any time for the same money. I must speak to him about that.

The early Market Harborough fairs were always busy; so much so that a few years after they began, when the number of evening school classes at the college increased, car parking became a real problem. With numerous evening classes and the toy fair all starting at 7pm, hundreds of cars would be descending on the college's decidedly limited car parking facilities at the same time. With no end of cars double-parked, others being driven onto the college playing fields and leaving tyre marks, and still more precariously parked down each side of the road, it was utter chaos.

Even after employing someone to help out as a car-parking steward, things were still difficult. Most people attending the toy fair would put up with it, but the evening class people were far from happy. One evening, one of the teachers stormed into the fair in a foul mood, demanding that things be sorted out. Because the fair was becoming so busy and the cars belonging to his students were being blocked in left right and centre, it was as he rightly said "A totally diabolical situation".

Eventually, we had no choice other than to give up the evenings and move the fair to Sundays. The weekend fairs worked well enough for a long time, but many people, with the possible exception of those attending evening classes, missed the atmosphere of those Wednesday evenings. Times change and most people now prefer going to bigger fairs. Even so, many will have fond memories of Market Harborough.

The first Toy and Train Fair at the Benn Hall in Rugby took place on a Sunday in 1980. Whether it was because there were not too many fairs about then, or we had hit just the right spot with an advert somewhere, I am not sure, but the place was heaving. This was before Sunday trading was legalised and although officially you were not supposed to trade on the Sabbath, the application of the law was inconsistent. As Sunday opening was not widespread and the places where people could shop were limited, any fairs allowed to take place could be extremely busy.

In some towns, trading on Sundays was fine, no problem at all. In others it was definitely taboo, whilst in a few it was perfectly in order unless or until members of the public complained. I am fairly certain that complaints must have been made here, although I don't recall the council officially telling us so. They simply informed us that we could no longer have Sundays, and in contrast to what had happened at Market Harborough, the fairs at Rugby were switched to Tuesday evenings.

Toy fairs at that time were more commonly known as swapmeets, but this was never a word we liked to use. It sounded all very cosy and friendly, and of course if you were used to going, you would know what to expect – you would know exactly what a swapmeet was. On the other hand, as far as the man in the street was concerned, our feeling was that either he wouldn't have a clue what the word meant or would assume it was some sort of club affair, almost certainly not for him anyway. Toy and Train Collectors Fair was, we felt, a better title.

Shortly after Rugby, fairs were added in Peterborough, Luton, Dunstable and Birmingham. The Birmingham venue was the Botanical Gardens in Edgbaston and a Wednesday evening fair was planned. Two interconnecting rooms were booked – the ballroom and a restaurant area, the latter having to be cleared in time for the fair. Given that it was to be an evening event, our fatal mistake was to view the place beforehand only during the daytime.

We opened at 7pm. It was a busy night and the tables set out in the ballroom were fine, but as the daylight began to disappear, the restaurant area became darker and darker – we had not reckoned on the subdued lighting. It would have been lovely had we been sitting down to a romantic dinner, but it was far from helpful for selling toys and after that first fair no one wanted to be stuck in the dark part. It was a pity really because the place had character (at least in daylight), people coming in would walk through a conservatory area past exotic plants. The lighting problem would not disappear, however, and after a few more fairs we moved to the Birmingham Anglers' Association's headquarters a couple of miles down the road.

The new Anglers venue worked well; great atmosphere and always packed. Most of the traders would re-book every time, which made the fair a very straightforward one to run. It was commonplace then for people to bring items along they wanted to sell. Bags of Dinky Toys and boxes of trains would be brought in at every fair, sometimes to swap, but more usually an advert for the fair in the local paper would spur people into clearing out their childhood toys.

I remember a man, having seen the ad in the paper, walking into the Birmingham fair one evening carrying a couple of boxes full of Hornby Dublo trains. We agreed a price, I paid him, and later, after I had returned home and was checking through what I had assumed all along to be just a box full of track, I found half a dozen boxed Dinky Toys including a Guy 'Spratt's' van lying at the bottom. Either the man was unaware that they were there or regarded them as having no value. Nowadays, when the average man in the street is likely to scrutinise anything that could be remotely classified as collectable, you just cannot imagine that sort of thing happening.

On another occasion there, a man told me he had a bus to sell. Walking outside with him, I assumed he had it in the back of his car, until I realised that his 'bus' was a real double decker in Birmingham colours parked right outside the front doors. It was not for me I hasten to add – I had suffered more than enough trouble from Marie about a 6ft 3inch model of a battleship perched on top of a wardrobe in our bedroom, so no way would I be contemplating anything even bigger. He can't have sold it that night, as shortly after I saw him he had to move it – there were complaints that it was blocking the road.

As the Anglers venue was always chock-a-block with stalls and visitors and there was no room to expand, eventually we needed to find somewhere with more space. We spent about eight years there, before re-locating the fair to the Clarendon Suite on Hagley Road, a larger venue able to accommodate 130 tables.

Dunstable's Queensway Hall was another very busy evening event and, just like Birmingham, there were not enough trestle tables on site. To make up the numbers we brought down about 70 of our own in a trailer van. We would arrive at the Queensway around 2pm, unload and set up, all of which made the fair hard work, but as we always had a hundred or more tables booked it was well worthwhile. At opening time there would be a long queue of people waiting to come in and very

A busy evening at Dunstable

soon the place would be a hive of activity. There was a toy fair there every two months for fifteen years and people such as Colin Penn, Bill Bourne, Arthur Ashard, John Butler and many more would never miss one. It was an excellent fair for everyone who came. For us though it was exhausting, and after we had taken all the tables down, packed them into the trailer van and arrived home around midnight, we just fell right into bed.

The whole Queensway building was an interesting 1960s futuristic design, with an oval shaped inner hall, and in its heyday it had been host to many big-name concerts and shows. The walls were wood panelled, and if you stood in the centre you could hear your voice echo. In later years, however, the place was beginning to show its age. It was badly in need of major refurbishment and overall use of the Queensway was declining.

When its demolition was threatened, there was strong local opposition, as there was simply no other exhibition or concert hall anywhere in Dunstable or its surrounding area. As in so many towns now, it is almost frightening to see just how much power and influence the retail giants have in local affairs, and after numerous meetings and discussions, they finally had their way. All the arguments for retaining and renovating the building were simply swept aside and it was a sad day when the Queensway was finally pulled down to make way for an Asda supermarket.

We could never find a replacement venue that was anything like as successful. A local school was fine for a time, but with so many people descending on the place just as evening classes were starting, exactly like Market Harborough years earlier, car parking became impossible. For a time we even used the Dunstable Leisure Centre just across the road from the old Queensway site, but it was never anything like as good as the old place.

One of our longest running fairs has been the Peterborough one at The Cresset in Bretton Centre. With regular traders such as Roy Lewin, Ken and the team from Dalesman Diecasts, Andy and Sue Howlett, Nigel Wiggins, John Garratt and Dave McDowall, the fair has always had a decent following. There was even an element of royal patronage for a time, when the Queen's cousin, the Duke of Gloucester, visited during the period he lived near Stamford. He must be one of the closest relatives of the Queen who can go about largely unrecognised, as he did for the most part at Peterborough. This was in complete contrast to the comedian Ernie Wise, who caused a bit of a stir when he popped in there one day.

The early 1980s saw the opening of the London Toy and Model Museum in Craven Hill, Paddington, founded with more than a little flair by Allen Levy and Narisa

Chakra. David Pressland, I believe, helped with some of the displays and in the early days the Curator was no less a person than Tim Armitage. As everyone who ever visited the London Museum will remember, there was a wonderful array of toys and trains on display.

One day I had called in to see Allen, when he asked me to join him for dinner in a restaurant nearby. Knowing Allen, I should have realised that there might have been a motive behind this welcome (but nevertheless unexpected) invitation. He fancied the idea of having a Toy Collectors Fair in the museum garden and asked if I would organise it. In truth the idea appealed just as much to me as it did to him, and we agreed to hold the fair on the forthcoming August Bank Holiday Monday. I would arrange it, pay the advertising costs, bring the tables down and have the stall money, whilst Allen would benefit from the admissions that additional visitors on the day would bring.

Out in the garden, there was not an inch of ground we didn't use. Stalls filled every nook and cranny – alongside the garden railway, around the children's roundabout, anywhere we could fit them in. People such as Peter Dunk, Richard Atkins, Roger Mazillius, Jeff Knight, Eric Cato, Mike Brown, Ken Simmons, Simon Goodyear and Pierce Carlson, whose very own apartment overlooked the garden, all had tables there. The sun was shining, there were some great toys around and it was a very pleasant day. The fair was popular with dealers and collectors alike and we continued to hold it one day each summer for the next few years.

Of course, being outside left us at the mercy of the weather and although we had some lovely sunny days in the garden, one or two others were decidedly damp. A few tables around the railway track had some protection, but for most of us if the heavens opened, as they did on one or two occasions, all we could do then was to hastily cover the stock and race into the museum café for shelter.

Opening a Toy Museum is a great idea, although I have always been of the opinion that unless you have a spot smack bang in the middle of a thriving tourist area, it cannot be too easy to make it pay from admissions alone. And there are a few souls about who might begrudge you even that.

A keen toy collector friend of mine, Norman Salt, together with his wife Annette, opened their museum in the early 1980s at Matlock Bath in Derbyshire. It was a labour of love. They spent forever getting everything set out, all the display cabinets installed and the whole place decorated from top to bottom. When all was complete it looked a treat – tin toys, trains, teddy bears, dolls and dolls houses; it was all very impressive. They set the admission price at a very reasonable 50p and were looking

The London Toy and Model Museum Fair

forward to the day of opening. When the big moment finally arrived, one of the very first men to come in paid his money, walked through then turned his head back to shout "50 pence! – All I want to do is look at 'em, not buy 'em." These Derbyshire lads must be a mean bunch – either that or someone had been down for the day from Yorkshire.

The only other fair we have ever arranged in an alfresco location was at the Great Central Railway in Loughborough. The fair was held on one or two Sundays in the summer on the platforms of the preserved station and, with steam trains running throughout the day, it had great atmosphere. The arrangement was similar to that at the London Toy Museum, whereby we looked after the advertising and other costs and collected the stall money, whilst the Great Central took and kept the admissions. In pleasant sunny weather, with the tables fully set up and steam trains pulling in and out, there was nowhere nicer to be. Even if it rained the tables were under the ornate Victorian platform canopy, which offered protection for most and

only a leak for those unlucky enough to have their table positioned under a broken roof pane.

To get the tables on site, we brought them down the day before in our trailer van to the far side of the track and then wheeled them by trolley for about two hundred yards over a crossing and up onto the platforms. The route we took with the tables was too lengthy for the stallholders to use, which meant that they had to hump their stock down the thirty steps from the Station's front entrance to the platform level. Of course at the end of the day, the same thirty steps had to be tackled once more – only this time uphill, not down. This, and the occasional black smuts shooting out from the steam engines and landing on the traders' stock, were the only drawbacks to the fair.

For a long time, as the Great Central day was always a busy one, intermittent black smuts and the odd damp day were grievances most stallholders would readily put

The Great Central Railway Fair

up with. They loved the event and we were usually fully booked with stalls. After a time though, when the novelty began to wear off a little and as some of the same guys were getting a bit older and going up and down those steps was getting a bit tougher, the stall bookings became harder to come by. Nevertheless, we had about fifteen very enjoyable years at the Great Central.

Peter Gurd is here – it must be opening time

ALL THE FUN OF THE FAIR

5

The bigger, the better

By the mid 1980s, Marie had left her Estate Agency job, my eldest son Simon had left school and the three of us were running the fairs together. Marie would look after the advertising side and the accounts, whilst Simon and I would do most of the physical work on the day of the fair, which was principally setting up the tables. Like myself, Simon began buying and selling toys and was running the fairs business alongside.

It was in the car driving down to London early in 1987 that Simon came up with the idea for one particular fair. The largest toy fairs at that time were the ones in Gloucester and Windsor, whilst Anthea Knowles had the London Toy Convention. Anthea's fair was a very stylish event, held in a succession of London hotels and we always enjoyed going there. It was a super show, with lots of foreign dealers and some great toys. The difficulties with access and parking in London, however, meant that it was never easy to attract visitors in large numbers.

Talking things over in the car, we came to the conclusion that a really large but good quality fair, not in central London, but somewhere on the outskirts could work well. Crucially though, wherever it was held would need to be somewhere easy to drive to and with enough parking on site for plenty of cars. We decided to start looking for somewhere to fit the bill and a number of venues were visited, including Alexandra Palace, although nothing felt exactly right until we discovered Sandown Park.

This seemed more like it – near to London and Heathrow, five miles from the M25, enough parking on site for thousands of cars, and a railway station nearby. Our only real concern was the size of the place. As the exhibition hall was far bigger than anything previously used for a toy fair, could we really fill it? Time alone would tell, so we went ahead and arranged the first date for Saturday 19th September 1987. Although there was room for even more, we decided to aim for four hundred tables. To get the message across strongly about the size, the advertising read '400 Stalls in one Superb Hall'. Once the flyers had gone out and adverts started to appear, we began to get some reaction from the traders. Irving Brim asked me not if the hall really was superb, but if I thought there were as many as four hundred people into taking stalls with toys and trains, and after a while I did begin to wonder.

The bookings were coming in steadily, but with maybe a month or so to go, we had about three hundred tables booked – still a hundred short. This was the first time we had ever quoted numbers of tables in adverts and it was beginning to worry me that perhaps we were unable to deliver what had been promised. I distinctly remember saying to Simon, that if we didn't get any more bookings, then we could always have a hundred tables stacked against the wall, so no one could complain that there were not four hundred in the hall.

Looking back now, I find it hard to believe that I even thought it, let alone said it. As if someone should walk in on the day and shout – "What's going on here then? I've counted up and there are only three hundred tables, not four hundred!" Was I seriously going to point to a mountain of wood piled up in one corner and say "No, that's just where you're wrong. Look – there's another hundred over there!" Of course I wasn't

In the end there was no need to panic. The table bookings were fine, the crowds swarmed in and the fair was busy all day long. There was a real buzz about the place and it was clear that the event was going very well. Towards the end of the day,

A good queue at Sandown

Lauren Bas from Holland with 'friend' at Sandown

people were telling us how much they had enjoyed the fair, which was all we ever wanted to hear. After that first event, the stall bookings became stronger each time, with the number of tables eventually expanding to the five hundred there are today. Sandown just hits the right mark and seems as strong now as ever. We will be fine there, unless of course you should ever bowl in one day and have to clamber

Sandown in full swing

over a hundred or so tables stacked up in the foyer – then you'll know we are in trouble.

Sandown Park attracts almost everyone dealing in and looking to buy old toys and so many of the stallholders have been coming here since the start. Mark Diamond, Dean Green, Roy Laycock, David Pressland, Ken Simmons, Mike Cooke, Lauren Bas, Marcus Krause, Vic Bailey, Jim Stevenson, Ron Ellis, Richard Atkins, Chris Graebe, Bob Field, John Martin, Dawn Allan, Mike Hobday, Peter Rumsey and Milan Simek are just a few of the regular faces. A number of others, no longer with us, were also regulars at Sandown – people like the train collector and expert repainter Maurice Launders and the collector and dealer Ken Hobday, although Ken's wife Wendy is still very much a regular with her dolls' houses.

I always liked Ken, a very friendly man and a keen train collector and it was obvious to everyone who knew him that he absolutely loved the buying and selling. One day at Gloucester, I was walking by his table when he shouted "Barry, I've got something here for you." It was an 0 gauge Exley or similar (as they like to say in the auction catalogues) Southern Railway Merchant Navy locomotive, a very nice thing. "How much?" I enquired, as I felt how heavy it was. "Eight," was his reply

Wendy Hobday at Sandown with her dolls' houses

and it got me seriously thinking, because I would have expected him to want well over a thousand. As Ken and I stood there talking, it gradually dawned on me without either the need or embarrassment of disclosing my hand that my 'eight' and Ken's 'eight' were two entirely different things. It was a question of noughts. Ken was in the big spender's league.

The only real problem I have at Sandown these days is that running it means that I don't really get to see the fair properly. For me, looking round at Sandown is as enjoyable as ever, but the only time I usually get to do that is late in the day. By that time I am no longer having to field questions about table positions, the location of the toilets, cars needing moving or whatever else, and so I am free to roam about a bit.

Sometimes you can even get a good deal late on, when someone does not want to take whatever it is back home again. More usually though, as I finally get to look around, I find it is a case of "Hello Barry – you should have seen me earlier, I had something you would have wanted." Or even worse "Just look at this I picked up this morning," as someone shows me an item I have been seeking for ages, which he has managed to find at a bargain price and from which he will not be parted.

Another satisfied customer

A very smartly attired Simon Goodyear

We turn up at Sandown on the Saturday morning around 6am, when there is invariably a line of vehicles already snaking from the exhibition gate right down to the road. Never mind the early starters though, one thing is for sure. If there was ever a prize awarded for who arrives last there could only ever be one winner. In this department, Simon Goodyear is the star performer in a class of just two, and has been so for years.

When Simon Goodyear and Peter Gurd are booked in at the same fair, it is always a close run thing and almost a bit of a competition to see which one is last to arrive. Mind you, Simon does not always play by the rules. Whereas Peter can arrive with just ten minutes, five minutes or even one minute to go, he is always sure to be on site when the fair is due to open. Simon, on the other hand, observes no such deadline and will often arrive when the fair is fully up and running. Whether he can claim a later arrival time somewhere else I am not sure, but at Sandown, where the opening time is 10.30am, I believe his record currently stands at 1.30pm. One line in the carol, Hark The Herald Angels Sing, is especially fitting for Simon – 'Late in time behold him come.'

Bob Field wins the 'Best Layout' shield at Rugby Vintage in 2006

Although the first fair at the Benn Hall in Rugby was back in 1980, another event was to spring up there four years later. The well known dealer, collector, train enthusiast and all round nice guy, John Ridley, unhappy that new models were becoming more and more prevalent at the fairs, wanted to turn the clock back to the early days when old toys and trains were the only ones around. As a result, in 1984 John started the Rugby Vintage Fair. As well as sales tables, there were working railway layouts and special displays. The event was a hit right from the start and became an annual fixture, usually on the first Saturday in September. John continued to organise the fair for about ten years, before handing the reins over to John Forman. That the fair became and has remained many people's favourite is a credit to them both. In 2001, John Forman decided to retire from organising the event and we were very pleased to pick up the baton.

Although we have tried to encourage a little more in the way of toys there in recent times, Rugby will always be considered a train event. Almost all the dealers at Rugby Vintage are permanent fixtures – people like Dean Green with his fabulous post-war Hornby 0 gauge and Peter Davies, Bob Field and Tony Cooper, three of the leading Hornby Dublo men. Likewise John Neale, Mike Delaney and Graham de Chastelain, three of the best-known dealers in 0 gauge trains. These and many others are always there. There are now two Rugby Vintage Fairs each year – the September one with layouts and displays as always and another in the early part of the year, without the layouts, but with more sales tables. The earlier fair gives more people the chance of having a table, as it can be difficult to find a place for many new people in September.

Someone on the waiting list once complained to me that his best chance of getting a table at Rugby would be if someone were to "drop off the perch". We are always doubly careful at Rugby to make sure that there are no boxes to trip over, no tables that might collapse or even any layouts wired up directly to the mains. All for Health and Safety reasons of course – we just don't want anyone dropping off that perch too early.

Rugby was not our first excursion into vintage toy fairs. In 1982 we staged a couple of vintage events at Lilford Hall in Northamptonshire. Mike Hobday, Peter Dunk, John Neale, Patrick Whitehouse, Jeff Knight, Simon Goodyear and many others came here and the fairs were very pleasant, if not unduly busy. The Lilford fairs were enjoyable enough, but there simply were not enough people through the doors for them to have a great future. It was a fine country house venue, and yet I suspect that the drawback with Lilford was its location – all very nice and picturesque, but really in the middle of nowhere.

Before the day of the first fair, a reporter and photographer from The Daily Telegraph, having heard the fair would be taking place, called in to see us about

With Simon, outside Lilford Hall in 1982

it. I think the newspaper's interest was to do with the fact that those everyday toys that we all had as kids were now becoming valuable. Collecting old toys can be viewed as a bit quirky anyway, which of course is always one of the media's favourite angles. What appeared in the paper was a huge close-up photograph of my head as I peered into a tin Citroën car, with my nose almost touching it (that's fairly quirky). Someone even had the nerve to suggest that this could have been the reason for the low attendance – seeing the picture had frightened people away. The very cheek of it.

The *Daily Telegraph* picture

Dennis and Freda Wright started the Buxton fairs in the Pavilion Gardens Concert Hall around 1980. In the early days we had the odd table there ourselves, so it had always been a fair familiar to us. This, together with the occasions when one or other of our regular stallholders had informed us that they were unable to book one of our fairs due to Buxton being on the same day, made us aware that the event had some pulling power. Consequently, when Dennis and Freda asked if we would like to take the fair over when they retired, we jumped at the chance. Buxton is a lovely town and the Victorian Concert Hall must be one of the most pleasant venues for a fair anywhere in the country.

The first Buxton fair we ran was just into the new Millennium, Sunday 2nd January 2000 to be precise. The doors opened at 10.30am and by 1pm the queuing still had not stopped. It became so busy inside that we had to close the doors and stop more people from coming in, until some already inside came out. It would be nice to imagine every fair being like that, although were it to be the case, then no doubt visitors would very soon complain about overcrowding. Doubtless the Health and Safety people would also have something to contribute, although I can already hear some stallholders saying they would take their chances. Buxton is usually busy, but that particular day was something else.

The Pavilion Gardens, Buxton

It is great when things work well, although a venue you feel sure would be exactly right for a fair can just as easily fail. Newbury Racecourse was a difficult one. A lovely new grandstand building, excellent lighting, easy access, acres of free parking and situated in an affluent area to boot, we were convinced it was a winner and arranged four dates for fairs there in 2002. As is often the case with a new event, everyone wants to give it a try and the table bookings for the first fair were strong. We had planned to use just the ground floor which accommodates 160 tables in comfort, but the telephone kept ringing with people wanting to come, and (let's be honest about it) turning business away is seldom if ever easy.

In the end, we elected to put another forty or fifty tables on the first floor, which to be fair was what any even modest estate agent would describe as very bright and airy with easy lift access. Now, I know full well that fairs on two levels can be a struggle, but I don't believe that was the reason for this one not taking off. We advertised strongly and everything seemed to be in place for a cracking first day. Just before 10.30am opening time, however, when we expected to see a good queue lining up outside, it wasn't really happening and we could sense no records were going to be shattered on the attendance side that day.

After an hour or so the hall was reasonably busy, although the atmosphere was a little flat and there was a general lack of urgency about the place. Indeed, checking the admissions later proved the attendance to be disappointing. It would not have been so bad if we could have pointed to a reason and said "OK, we made the mistake of doing this or not doing that" but we couldn't. Anyhow, reflecting on the fair and faced with the low number of re-bookings, we regretted having booked and advertised three further dates for Newbury.

Cancelling any fair, we have always believed, should be an absolute last resort that is undertaken only when there is just no alternative, otherwise it can put a question mark over everything else you do. The telephone rings often enough as it is, without every single person feeling that they had better call to check if such and such a fair really is on, because they heard the one at Newbury last week was cancelled. Our feeling is that unless something happens out of our control forcing us to cancel, we just have to carry on. The next three fairs at Newbury were already advertised in our programme, so we persevered.

Needless to say, both stall bookings and the numbers through the door at Newbury continued to fall. A fair on the decline can represent a double whammy. Not only is there now every chance of losing money, but it can also be tricky to keep the event looking respectable, in terms of table numbers, for those people who do make the effort to attend. We did the best we could, but it was hard going. Financially, as we

Toys for young and old at Buxton

had made money on the first fair that profit went some way to make up for losses on the later ones. We were not sorry though when the whole thing was finally put to bed.

Probably the first fair we had which did not succeed was in Cambridge back in 1982. Although the Kelsey Kerridge Sports Centre was near the town centre where parking was a permanent headache, it was integrated into a large multi-storey car park which seemed perfect for stallholders and visitors alike. We had flyers printed to boost the first fair and Simon spent about two hours the day before, placing one under the wiper blade of every car parked in the same multi-storey.

Convinced that this was going to bring in a whole crowd of new customers, we were just about to open the doors and let the fun begin when the attendant from the multi-storey strolled in to see us. "These must be yours," he declared with a grin, plonking down a thick wad of our flyers he had carefully removed from every single windscreen in the car park. His face said it all. Leaflets on cars was something he was not going to tolerate on his patch. The fair was not a disaster, but neither was it a brilliant success, there were simply not enough people coming in. Naturally, we blamed that car park attendant. Even without him, however, it is a fair bet that it would not have made a scrap of difference.

The Stoneleigh fair ran for about ten years. The first couple of events here were held in what were really agricultural buildings, although we thought it best not to include any such description in our advertising. In fact the Stoneleigh management obviously took the same view over their venue's marketability, as in all correspondence and discussions with us, the building was always referred to as an 'Exhibition Hall'.

It was only when we called at the security gate to collect the keys to the 'Exhibition Hall' that Stoneleigh's management's true perception of one of its rentable properties fully emerged. The keys we required were firmly attached to a large wooden fob on which was inscribed in large letters 'Cow Sheds'.

The fairs in the sheds were busy enough, with plenty of tables booked and visitors coming in. Even after hiring no end of large gas heaters though, it was still a cold place and to be frank, slightly on the grim side. The sheds were really a temporary measure that we used whilst the new exhibition hall was being built and as soon as we were given the green light to transfer there, we moved in right away.

There was space in the new hall for 300 tables and things went along very nicely for a good few years. The public attendance here, very much like the table bookings, was good rather than great. Stoneleigh worked well enough up to a certain level, although due no doubt to its slightly off the beaten track location, it was never easy to get the fair really heaving with visitors. On the tables side we generally had a decent number booked, without managing to fill the place completely.

All of this 'real world' experience was very much in our minds in 2002, when the Stoneleigh management, in their infinite wisdom, informed us of their new plans. Beginning in 2003, they had taken the view that all fairs must be held – there was to be no debate about it – in a newly built hall twice the size and costing twice the price of the current one. Given this fait accompli, unless we felt that losing money on every fair from then on at Stoneleigh would be an amusing thing to do, there was not much thinking needed. The time had finally come to throw in the towel.

A few years earlier, but some years after we had started to run the Stoneleigh fairs, the Coventry Diecast Club had asked us if we would like to take over the fair they had been running at the Sports Connexion. The venue was a pleasant one, plenty of free parking and with very easy access. Taking the fair on and running both it and Stoneleigh for a time made an interesting comparison and contrast. The two places can have been only eight miles or so apart, but because Stoneleigh was always perceived by stallholders and visitors alike as a much bigger event, we could never get anywhere near the same number of people through the doors at the Connexion.

In exactly the same way, those smaller fairs of ours like Market Harborough, Northampton and Luton, all ones which worked well enough at one time or another, have now sadly had their day. Just as the big supermarkets and the huge out of town stores are appealing, there is no doubt that many people nowadays adopt exactly the same philosophy about fairs – simply "the bigger the better".

Ten years ago, when anyone called enquiring about a fair, they would probably ask what time it started, or how to get there or maybe they would want to know what type of things would be for sale. Now the first question more often than not is "How many tables will there be?" Of course there are a few smaller fairs that will continue to work, but it is true to say that anything just starting up will almost certainly need to be either big or very specialised to have any chance of succeeding in the long term.

Anyone who has ever revisited his or her first school, the one all of us started at four or five years of age, will tell you how small everything there now looks. All those buildings and classrooms that were huge when we were knee high to a grasshopper, now seem tiny. Seeing things differently as a child of course is understandable, but walking around Stratford upon Avon not long ago, Marie and I had a far more recent 'then and now' comparison. We stopped by, not the Leisure Centre, but the hall where John Curtis held his original toy fair in the town and where we had taken sales tables ourselves on occasion. I always liked John, he was an outgoing, larger than life character, who among other things was a Children's Entertainer and a Toastmaster.

The hall he used for his Stratford Fair was on the cosy side at the best of times, but the tables we occupied there were in a sort of side annexe next to the windows. Peering through those same glass panes now, the place did not merely look small – it was positively minute. We just could not believe how John had managed to get away with fitting those tables in. We calculated that, with the trestles in place, about eighteen inches would be left over for the public aisle. Just try doing that today, with the Health and Safety people breathing down your neck. One look at that set up and forget a reprimand or even a fine – you would probably be marched away and locked up, no messing. I had remembered it being tight in there, but not that tight. Knowing John, he would no doubt have said it lent the place atmosphere. Maybe it was that he had in mind when he said to me one day "You know me Barry – I'm in the entertainment business."

Kettering has been a decent fair now for some years. The hall is a large one and stallholders such as Bill Bourne, Brian Baker, Keith Hadley, Richard Taylor, Ray Martin, Bob Andrews and many others are regulars and the fair works well. Our last event there for 2006 was held on Sunday 12th November, which was also Remembrance Day and naturally we wanted to observe a two-minute silence at 11am. Unfortunately, the public address system was out of action, and as the fair would be opening at 10.30am and by 11am there would (hopefully) be a lot of people in the hall, the problem was one of attracting everyone's attention.

On the first floor is a balcony overlooking the entire hall. The perfect vantage point from which to address everyone below, but as I was uncertain as to whether my voice was going to be strong enough to silence the crowd, I asked the Leisure Village manager if she knew anyone else that could shout louder. "Oh yes," she said, "Ernst is the man, I will go and get him." He duly came and sure enough, he was a big man with a powerful voice. "I could do it", he said "But I had better not." "Why not?" I asked. "Because I'm German," he answered. As soon as the words had left his lips, I realised that the image of him, even with only the slightest trace of a German accent, standing on that balcony on Remembrance Day and barking orders down to everyone below would have been far too much to handle. It could have made 'The Germans' episode in Fawlty Towers pale into insignificance.

"However" he said, "I do have a whistle." This was the answer. The two of us stood together on the balcony and at 11am precisely he blew the whistle long and hard, exactly as would be done in similar circumstances before a football match. It silenced the whole place immediately. This allowed me to shout "Two Minutes Silence Please!" From then, until be blew the whistle again two minutes later, you could have literally heard a pin drop. It was the perfect Anglo-German operation.

When it comes to running a fair, after the cost of hiring the venue, advertising is where most of the expenditure goes. Almost everything we go through life paying money for, be it cars, clothes, holidays or whatever, we can usually take a judgement afterwards on how wise our spending has been. If a hotel we stayed in proved not to our liking, we wouldn't go there again. On the other hand, if we found a particular bottle of wine we liked, the next time we might buy a case. We simply get to know what works for us. When it comes to advertising, however, especially for a public event like a fair, knowing whether money has been well spent can be one of life's classic imponderables. That big ad looked really good in the local paper, but how do you ever really know whether the £500 spent on it brought one more person through the door?

John Wanamaker, who is considered to be the father of the modern department store and indeed modern advertising was quoted as saying "I know that half of my advertising dollars are wasted....I just don't know which half." Currency differences aside, I could not have put it better.

Specialist magazines like Collectors Gazette we feel we have to advertise in. With these publications, maintaining an image can be just as important as any efforts to attract new people. Even if now and again you might feel that you are preaching to the converted, people expect to see you there and would probably begin to wonder whether things were going down the pan if you were not.

No, it is the effectiveness of ads placed in local newspapers, and anywhere else where you hope to attract fresh people from, that can be difficult to gauge. At the end of the day, just how many new people advertising in these areas actually pulls in is more guesswork than anything else. We tend to go fairly strongly in the local papers. If nothing else it gives us peace of mind, knowing that 'the advertising has been done' as it were. It means that if we were ever to open the doors at a fair and see no one walk through, at least we could sleep that night feeling we had done our job. Whether the traders would quite see it that way of course is another matter entirely.

Many years ago, Simon and I had a table at a fair in Shrewsbury organised by someone no longer on the scene. Shrewsbury, it seems to me, is a very nice town a long way from anywhere, except perhaps Wales. It was certainly a long way from us. We arrived, set up the sales table in eager anticipation and when the doors opened, six people walked in. At the end of the day after the number through had risen to about fifty, the organiser, a very nice man, came round to see us. To his credit, he was genuinely very sorry that the event had not worked and said "I can't understand it, I really can't. I've spent £30 advertising this fair".

There is one thing about newspaper advertising that is a certainty. Once you are seen to be a regular advertiser, you are then a sales target for every rival newspaper in the area trying to sell space. It is amazing how many times they call and have just one prime space left before they go to press, and there is always a special price just for you. There is the really pushy sales person who starts the conversation like they are your best friend, but who clearly does not understand the word 'No'. You can put up with that, it is their job after all, but what really gets me is when the best mate chat is done, they finally concede defeat, say goodbye and immediately click the phone off with a finger and you are left with the dialling tone buzzing in your ear. It is just so insulting. I am amazed they are not trained to avoid doing it.

As well as the newspapers, from time to time we experiment with different magazines. Only recently, we spent about £400 on a half page advertising the Sandown Park Fair in one of the glossy teddy bear magazines we had not previously tried. In an effort to encourage more teddy people, who had perhaps not been to Sandown, the wording in the ad clearly stated free admission for one or two people if they brought the ad along with them. This, we reasoned, was the one true way the effectiveness of the new ad could be put to test, albeit at what could be quite a cost. At the close of the fair and after thousands of people had been through the doors, we counted exactly fourteen free admission ads, relating to a maximum of twenty-eight people. Even then, who is to say some of those twenty-eight would not have been coming anyway?

ALL THE FUN OF THE FAIR

6

What's the weather like?

Fairs are usually busier during the winter months, when people are not distracted with summer activities like holidays, gardening or an outside event going on somewhere or other. Those things do not usually interfere in the colder parts of the year, when the only outside influence you really have to worry about then is the weather. Nowadays of course with the advent of round the clock television, the weather is a big news item and the way the media go out of their way to report anything remotely resembling bad conditions is crazy.

The reason for this can be traced back precisely to 1987, when the met office was severely criticised for failing to warn us about the hurricane hitting the south east of England. As a result, ever since then they have worked on the basis of always telling us that things are going to be bad. This for them is a 'win every time' policy. If they are proved right and the weather is nasty – no problem, they have done their job. On the other hand, if the weather is actually OK, they know they won't be hauled over the coals because everyone will just be so relieved.

As far as snow is concerned, the way they talk about it now, you would think we had never seen any before. It is like the end of the world is coming. When you see a weather reporter on television against a background of falling snow, it is usually in the far north of Scotland and they omit to tell you that everywhere else in Britain is perfectly clear. As far as we are concerned, all this would be amusing if we didn't have a fair to run the next day. In a situation like that, the very last thing you want to hear at the end of the weather report is "Don't travel unless it's absolutely necessary." Of course there will be occasions when it is only right and proper to say that, but the number of times you hear that message and then find that the weather is perfectly fine, is simply ridiculous.

Very few fairs of ours have been affected by snow, although there is one deserving of a mention. We first went to look at the Reebok Stadium near Bolton in the summer of 2000. Right next to the motorway, near to Manchester and the whole Northwest conurbation, it seemed a perfect venue for a toy fair. We arranged the

The publicity picture used for the first Reebok Stadium Fair

first date to fit into the period between Christmas and the New Year, Thursday 28th December 2000. All the advertising was in place, coloured posters and flyers had been printed and the stall bookings had been strong. There was a good feeling about the whole thing.

Simon, Ellis and I had driven up the day before and checked into the De Vere Hotel in the stadium complex for that evening. After setting up the tables for the fair, we had dinner and retired to bed. The weather was cold but dry, although the forecast had mentioned snow the next day. Our rooms faced inside the stadium overlooking the football pitch and when we awoke about 5am, the once green turf was now completely covered in a white blanket. Worse than that, the white stuff was coming down heavily with two or three inches already on the ground. At any other time we would have enjoyed looking out at this lovely winter scene, but with a 250-stall fair to run we failed to appreciate its beauty. We dressed, had breakfast and made our way into the exhibition hall, having no idea how many people would eventually be joining us.

From about 7am onwards my mobile phone started ringing, with Marie telling me about stallholders who had called to say they were snowed in. After a while, the first of those people who could get through started to arrive. With the bad weather, the car-parking stewards we had arranged to be there had not turned up, so we were outside directing traffic ourselves. In the snow, it was impossible to see the outline of the access road through to the unloading doors, and, as it was the very first fair at the Reebok, no one would be sure of exactly where to go. We guided the early arrivals in, leaving tracks in the snow, which people coming along later could follow. On top of everything else, I finished up slipping over, landing awkwardly and fracturing my right arm at the elbow. It was definitely a first fair to remember at the Reebok Stadium.

Looking out at the snow that morning, we feared that the day would be a disaster. In the event we had around a hundred stallholders turn up and nearly fifteen hundred people through the doors, which given the conditions was remarkable. It told us two things. Firstly, that people in the north are a hardy bunch who don't go into hibernation as soon as a bit of bad weather shows its face. Secondly, in more normal conditions there should be plenty of good fairs to look forward to at the Reebok. We have had a lot of wet and windy weather up there since that day and even a bit more snow, but the fairs have been great. Always plenty of stalls and a long queue of people waiting to come in. You really cannot ask for much more.

The Reebok Stadium fair under way

In January 2005 we took over the Stafford Showground fair from Pat and Roger Minkley. Although we had never visited when Pat and Roger's fair was running, just like Buxton we knew it was one attracting good support. The Showground itself we had travelled to on occasion for other events such as car shows and antiques fairs, but I think what interested us most about the venue was its having been host to two separate large antiques fairs for such a long time. During a period when some antique events elsewhere could struggle, it suggested that there should be the potential for a good public attendance.

Stafford is a very straightforward fair to run. The venue is well lit, there are acres of car parking space and access for the stallholders is easy enough. With two adjoining halls in use there now and usually a good crowd of customers through the doors, the fair works very well. Sometimes there is even an antiques fair in progress in another hall, which a lot of people seem to like as they can visit both shows on the same day. The problem for me is that Marie is one of them and that might mean some spending on her part, so for a Yorkshireman it is a bit of a mixed blessing.

Early in 2005, driving along the M6 motorway near to Coventry, we had begun to notice a new stadium taking shape, strikingly similar to the Reebok we knew so well. Driving nearer for a closer look, it was clear that there was plenty of construction work still to do, but the building looked impressive. The stadium management team were working from portable buildings on site and they told us that a large exhibition hall was planned for the complex. Marie, Simon, Ellis and myself arranged to go over for an inspection and after each of us had donned a hard hat, a very helpful lady took us on a tour inside. The outer shell of the stadium was more or less complete. Internally though, it was all breeze blocks and heavy machinery with dozens of contractors working away. Standing there looking at plans, it was hard to imagine where things like walls and entrance and unloading doors were going to be. Nevertheless, it looked exactly right for a really big fair.

It was of course the Ricoh Arena and, just like the Reebok Stadium, there was a large adjacent shopping precinct and, being a football stadium, thousands of parking spaces. Best of all, it was right next to the M6 motorway and within easy reach of Coventry, Birmingham and the whole of the West Midlands. The hall was big and after measuring up – and without needing to use John Curtis of Stratford fame's formula for working out the aisle widths – we found that it would accommodate 500 tables in comfort.

Although the stadium was not finished, we wanted to have the first fair arranged as soon as possible. The problem with construction work of course, as we all know from just having the builders in at home, is the genuine risk of delay. It was

Ellis at The Ricoh Arena during construction

tempting to set a first date towards the end of 2005 when the stadium was scheduled to be ready, although thinking it through we came to the conclusion that it was better to be safe than sorry. This was fortunate, as we would have been in trouble going any earlier and the first fair was arranged for Sunday 29th January 2006.

The response from stallholders to the fair was terrific. This was great, but not totally unexpected, as we knew well enough from the Newbury experience that most traders do like to try out a new fair. At the end of the day, for the event to be a lasting success, it was all going to hinge on getting plenty of visitors through the doors. The fair was due to open at 10.30am and just before then, I walked outside to see how things were shaping up. I couldn't see the end of the queue. It was out of sight around the corner of the stadium, which was a good sign. The whole day went extremely well and it was pleasing to have a lot of very positive comments from both visitors and stallholders. The Ricoh Arena Fair, it seemed, was here to stay.

Fairs have changed a lot since the first Market Harborough one back in 1979, when virtually every table was full of old toys and trains. The only new items then, apart

The Ricoh Arena fair

from 00 gauge trains, were Models of Yesteryear. Unlike the early very collectable Yesteryears from the 1950s and 1960s, the only thing ever to change on the ones produced from the middle 1970s onwards was the lettering. When you consider how basic these things were – no end of different transfers or decals applied to the same castings and every model presented in an identical, uninspiring see-through panel box – it is no wonder that they are not so popular now. These simple models are light years away from anything produced today.

At most fairs nowadays, new models are in the majority and when you look at the range and quality of them, you can understand it. Most are made in China and other eastern places of course, but as long as we have an active input into the design, the distribution and the retail side, why should it matter? The fact is that the accuracy and quality of the models produced today (and even the attractive packaging they come in) can hardly be bettered.

Something that has not changed at the fairs is the fun it can be. It was that friendly, relaxed atmosphere where people were out to enjoy themselves that first struck me when I started visiting fairs, still working for a living as it were in the outside world. It is exactly the same today. Collectors go to a fair to see what they can buy, to meet up with fellow enthusiasts, and to have an enjoyable day out, while the dealers are working at something they really want to do.

Of course as a full time dealer, when your living depends on selling, the sums have to add up, but anyone doing something they really enjoy will try even harder to make it work than they would with a normal job. At most fairs, even the bigger ones, stallholders know many of their customers and as well as the buying and selling it is the banter between them and the shared interests in the trains or models that can be fun. As a stallholder or a collector, going to a fair where you know either your friends or other people with similar interests will be, is a nice thing. It is certainly what makes running the fairs enjoyable for us.

With mid-week evening fairs and all the ones at the weekends, other than Christmas Day and Boxing Day (although I seem to recall the latter being used once or twice), there is rarely a day in the year now without a toy fair going on somewhere or other. Many stallholders are out every weekend and perhaps once or twice mid-week as well, so there can be a lot of travelling to do. One very active dealer in diecast models is Tony Evans from the West Midlands. As well as running his stall, Tony is a great help to us in setting up the tables at many of the fairs, including Stafford Showground, the Reebok Stadium, the Ricoh Arena, and Sandown Park. Very often Tony will arrive at a fair before we do, and when you think that we can be at the Reebok Stadium before 6am or at Stafford around 5am, this takes some dedication.

Tony is the most prolific and consistent stallholder at toy fairs I know. Sure, a few people might book more tables than Tony, but I know of no one who will attend more fairs. Tony is perhaps not quite as frequent a traveller as he once was, but for a long time, from Chester-le-Street in County Durham to Exeter and from Carlisle to Sittingbourne in Kent, in a single year Tony often attended around 250 fairs. There cannot be many toy events, if any, that Tony has not tried and his record for continuous trading is having tables at no less than 22 fairs on consecutive days.

Even though it might not be his appetite for driving the length and breadth of the country every week, if there is something I definitely do share with Tony, it is his views about collecting. As Tony rightly says, some people get far too obsessed when buying toys, especially diecast, over whether their purchase will be a good investment. When all is said and done, how much does it really matter whether an item bought now is going to be worth more or less in ten or twenty years time? Is

Tony Evans – standing still for once

it not enough to have the pleasure of owning the model now and know that in the future it will definitely be worth something?

Thousands of collectors enjoy themselves every week of the year looking around at fairs, seeing what is about and buying the models they want – and at the end of the day, they have something tangible to show for it. Not only that, but with the competitive element you find at the fairs nowadays, especially when it comes to recent diecast and trains, there is usually no cheaper place to buy.

When it comes to spending money on a hobby, anyone who goes to watch football, play golf, drink down at the pub, or indulge in most other leisure activities, will have a good time right enough, but other than the memory of it they will return with nothing. How much of an investment is that exactly?

A DEALER'S LIFE FOR ME

7

Are you a collector or a dealer?

I have come to realise that the years I spent buying and selling toys and trains, and it was mainly trains, were some of the best and most enjoyable I have ever had. I had a great time, working really hard when it suited, having time off when it suited and making lots of friends.

It is strange really how we tend to talk about dealers and collectors as being two entirely separate breeds, for when it comes to toys and trains, almost without exception, dealers are themselves among the most serious of collectors. It is their very collecting that will have brought almost all of them into the business of buying and selling in the first place and most of them are passionate about what they do. For them, it is a bit like being a kid let loose in a sweet shop, never mind a toy shop. What could be better than to be making a living, totally involved every day with the things that interest you the most? Dealers are the people who really know about toys and trains, handling these items all the while and building up expert knowledge and opinion on all the important factors such as originality, rarity, condition and desirability.

There are so many nice people about who buy and sell toys and trains for a living. Dealers are relied on by so many collectors to come up with the items they need – they can advise over what or what not to buy, about particular items coming up for sale privately or through an auction, and their expertise can be invaluable. Increasingly nowadays when it comes to the more specialised or expensive items, dealers will have customers whose likes and wants are noted and will act as the collector's eyes and ears in the search for what is required.

After saying all that, not everyone looks upon dealers so favourably. It is a long time since I was buying and selling trains, and perhaps as some of the older collectors become less active and new people come onto the scene, the way in which dealers are regarded might be changing a little. Nevertheless, as collectors have so many differing views on the subject, I thought it might be interesting to explore the way in which dealers are sometimes perceived.

In my buying and selling days, the attitude some people had towards anyone engaged in such activity was a source of continual amazement to me. No matter how well you might have treated your customers, how fairly your business was conducted or how highly you might have been regarded elsewhere, in some people's eyes, if you were a dealer you could never really do the right thing. For a start, as far as some collectors' buying activities were concerned, with a dreaded dealer on the prowl, they felt that their chance of acquiring whatever it was cheaply would be coming under threat.

Before I was ever into buying toys, I remember being in auction rooms and whenever an antiques professional would walk through the door, you would often hear something like "Look out! The dealers are here – just watch the prices now." Among a few people there is an underlying feeling of resentment towards the dealer, based on what they as a collector look upon as a hobby being regarded by the dealer as a business. Mostly their dislike of dealers hinges on the profit element. As far as they are concerned, if a dealer has bought something for £100 and sold it for £110, someone somewhere has been done out of a tenner.

The same person, however, walking into any shop and buying say a pair of shoes, a television set or even an expensive watch would never worry for a second that the retailer has paid one price and is selling at another. With the goods we all buy every day of our lives, there is an acceptance among us all that this is the way things are done – retailers need to make a profit.

The problem lies not with toys and trains per se, but with trading in second-hand items in general and anything of an antique or collectable nature in particular. It is to do with the fact that the item in question has already been out there in the public domain and is now considered fair game. Unlike a brand new product, which travels down the route of manufacture, wholesale and then into a retail shop – a route strictly out of bounds to the man in the street – this old toy or train has been out in the big wide world actually belonging to someone.

What niggles away at some people is the thought that, if only they or some other collector out there might have been a bit luckier, they could have bought it for the same price as the dealer. It is the thought that, no matter what price the dealer is asking, it has to be more than the person who sold it in the first place received. The fact that whoever sold it to the dealer may have had it passed down through the family for nothing, or even bought it years ago for £50 and has now ended up with £500 is not considered relevant – as that person is not a dealer.

If the same person who is averse to dealers were selling a collection, he or she would undoubtedly like it to be sold directly to a collector. They will assume that whatever price is offered by a dealer it cannot be enough, because after all the collection is to be sold again. Surely, they reason, there must be a better price to be had from a collector? On the face of it, this might sound a reasonable assumption – is it not far better to sell to the end user? In reality, the chances of whoever is selling being able to locate a collector who would be a strong buyer for every single item they have are, in my experience, remote.

As a dealer in buying situations, I always wanted to wear my dealing hat and treat the whole thing as a commercial transaction. This was my job after all, and I didn't want the fact that I happened also to be a collector to cloud the issue. If I was buying from collectors I knew, or from others who had some knowledge of current values, there wasn't usually a problem. Sure, our thoughts might differ on a few things, but generally speaking an agreement would be reached without too much trouble.

On the other hand, I can recall so many occasions when I would go along to look at a collection of toys or trains and the person selling would ask me whether I was a collector or a dealer. With some people I could sense it was almost like asking whether I was good or bad, a saint or a sinner. Was I going to pay a 'collectors price', even though they were often not sure what that was, or a 'dealer's price' which they assumed could be bettered in an instant by any collector plucked out from a crowd at random?

It was the assumption some people had that any collector out there (no matter how casual or low key their approach to collecting), just because they were seen as someone who would be keeping these things themselves, would be guaranteed to pay more than the most committed dealer.

The truth is that even the keenest and wealthiest of collectors will only ever pay strong prices for the particular items they want. Most collectors who are offered a wide range of items outside of their definite 'wants list' will only be lukewarm at best when it comes to paying good prices. Specialist dealers, who are in any way serious about what they are doing, will have access to the best buyers for special pieces and will be well placed to present everything else that comes along in the wider market place. Consequently when it comes to buying, particularly a large collection, specialist dealers can and usually will pay more than most collectors.

As well as the financial side of things, the collector versus dealer issue can also raise its head when it comes to people wanting to feel that their treasured possessions are going to a person or place where they will be appreciated. I have heard so many people over the years say "I'd like my toys to go to a good home." What do they mean by a good home? A bank vault that offers total protection? Someone who will keep these toys in their boxes, look at them occasionally, and promise never to play with them? I could understand the sentiment in principle, but I had no idea what it meant for that individual seller in practice and, very often I suspect, neither did they.

I can understand people wanting to pass items from their collection onto special friends. They might have in mind someone they like who has always taken a shine to a particular piece, or a fellow collector they want to reward who has been helpful in some way. I don't want to sound mercenary, but except for instances such as these, why should anyone need to worry about precisely where their collection will finish up? The fact is that in today's strong collecting market, wherever the items go they will most certainly be valued and wanted.

I used to detect a feeling among some people, that items bought by a dealer would somehow not be looked after quite so well as those sold directly to a collector. As though the dealer, whose very living depended on presenting these things in their best possible condition to a customer, could not care less. It is a view that has always struck me as naïve. No matter whether the collection is acquired by a dealer or a collector, every single item in it will become part of another treasured collection eventually. As far as 'going to a good home' is concerned, with the prices these things are worth nowadays, you have to ask yourself – when are they really ever going to go to a bad one?

Ultimately, of course, when all is said and done, we are only ever custodians of these things. No matter how deeply we feel that we would never part with certain special items or even our whole collection, the inescapable fact is that someone else will own our toys one day. I mentioned that to a friend of mine recently, and added that at the end of the day we can't take these things with us. He probably spoke for more than a few of us when he said, "In that case, I'm definitely not going."

When it comes to dealing in toys and trains, three stalwarts (and fellow Yorkshiremen to boot) regularly come to mind. Their names, which appear in strict alphabetical order please note, as I would not want to imply any notion of seniority in either expertise or indeed age, are Tim Armitage, Simon Goodyear and John Haley. Most of us naturally tend to show a little extra deference and respect to those people who have been in the same business longer than ourselves, and there is no doubt that these three can make me look like a mere newcomer. These three very nice guys (you see, I can't help it) have seemingly, in my eyes at least, been around forever.

If I dare to include myself in this exalted company for a moment, I am not sure quite what it proves (unless there really is something in the Yorkshire water) but, of the three of us in that quartet who are married, each has a son named Simon. Conversely the one who is not and who therefore does not, is himself called Simon.

I first came across Tim Armitage at his shop in Leeds in the very early 1970s. Tim's shop was on the high level of the County Arcade which, as he mentioned to me recently, cost £5 a week to rent. I cannot recall too much about the shop, for even though I was interested in trains, I was not in a position to buy. Tim does not remember my only visit there, which given the circumstances is hardly surprising. I had a lead toy cannon that I tried to sell to him. He asked me if I had dug it up, which struck me as an unusual approach – maybe he had a preference for toys that had been buried, I wasn't sure. The more likely suggestion, however, was that he might not be paying me a fortune for it. This latter view turned out to be the more accurate, as he didn't want my cannon at any price and I took it home again.

After Leeds, Tim's next shop was in Batley, which must be remembered with affection by many older collectors as he had so many good toys and trains, particularly trains, for sale. I did pay a couple of visits there, although I cannot recall actually buying anything. I do remember him having a full rake of Milbro 0 gauge private owner wagons on a top shelf, but there were so many nice things for sale. Tim has been buying and selling toys since the 1960s and will have seen most things over the years. There will have been so much back then that he would have dismissed at the time as being readily available, or that no one really wanted which might now be making big money, but that is just the way things go. Even so, Tim has a good feel for very early toys and is an avid collector and dealer in nineteenth and early twentieth century commercially made trains, of which he has some fine examples.

Simon Goodyear, I believe, began his train career in Chuffs train shop in London. I never knew the place, although I understand it was a real emporium. Over the years he has acquired a great knowledge of toy and model trains and is a particular expert on products of the Leeds Model Company. My first sighting of Simon must have been in his shop in Huddersfield. In similar fashion to Tim's in Leeds, Simon's shop was located high up in a town centre arcade. Rather than simply being on the first floor, however, Simon went one better and had his emporium two storeys up.

I dare say with a specialist shop you would not necessarily need to be on the high street, as the keen people would always search you out. After saying that, those two flights of stairs must have sorted out the men from the boys, or maybe the serious buyers from the time wasters. If you made it up to the top you wouldn't want to go away empty handed, although I for one probably did. I don't remember seeing a lift, so if you have ever wondered how Simon has managed to remain so slim, all those years of carting the stock up the stairs might have something to do with it.

John Haley has been dealing in toys since goodness knows when, maybe even he has forgotten how long. It was only in relatively recent times, however, perhaps twenty years or so ago, that he and his son Simon opened their shop in Halifax. To be fair, it is Simon who runs the shop, described in advertisements as 'One of the best stocked shops of old toys in the world', which can be no less than the truth. The stock is obviously the most important part of any shop, although definitely of note in this one are the cases in which it stands. Beautifully shaped in wood and glass, they must have been rescued from a gentlemen's outfitters or drapers and are worth visiting the shop to see.

John and I never met whilst Marie and I lived in Yorkshire, but as long as I have known him he has always had the same very laid back approach. It is one I feel sure has been developed from years of experience with a view to putting you off your guard. I have always felt that John would make a very good poker player; perhaps he already is. Either way, one thing is for certain – if you show him a toy you feel sure will be right up his street, he will always respond with an air of calm indifference. Then, just when you think, "Well, perhaps he isn't too bothered after all," he will go in for the close when you least expect it. Whenever we lesser mortals are offered something we desperately want to acquire, we would usually find it well nigh impossible to hold our enthusiasm in check, but John is a master at it. He is known all over the world for toys, especially his speciality mechanical toy banks and he knows his subject very well.

It would not be the done thing to pass over those Yorkshiremen of the toy and train world without mentioning David Thackeray. David is not a dealer but a collector of, and an authority on, 0 gauge trains made by such companies as Leeds, Milbro, Exley and Bonds. Just like John Hayley, David has a habit of not wanting to appear too eager over anything that could be a potential purchase. On the other hand, whenever he has anything to sell, it is hard to imagine anyone able to muster more enthusiasm. As David will tell you, it will be the best piece on the market and we should all be grateful we are even offered the chance of it. David is a lot of fun. He too has a son named Simon.

A DEALER'S LIFE FOR ME

8

The fun of the deal

During the late 1970s and the 1980s, Gloucester and Windsor were the main toy fairs. There was great atmosphere at both, which started not just when the doors were opened for stallholders to set up, but in the car park outside.

Windsor was organised then as it is today by The Maidenhead Static Model Club, and was regarded as the leading fair for diecast. I always enjoyed going there – parking up and looking round at anything for sale out in the car park, before doing the same inside the hall.

When it came to the doors being opened for stallholders to set up, at I believe 9.30am sharp, everyone had to squeeze through one small door. First thing in the morning, with perhaps 200 people just itching to get in, set up their stands and whizz around the hall looking to buy, having to slowly filter through this bottleneck was forever frustrating. That aside, it was a great fair and still is.

For most of the time I went down to Windsor, there were more people wanting tables than there were tables available. I had two booked here for a long time and as I didn't want to miss out, I would religiously re-book for the next fair whilst on site. Bookings were made at the front desk during a specified time slot, which I seem to remember ended at 3pm. Lynn Kenwood was the person taking the bookings on the day I had forgotten about the time moving swiftly along, and I walked up to pay about ten minutes past three.

"Too late now," declared Lynn "You'll have to send it in." "Who do I send it to?" I asked, standing there with the money visible in my hand. "Send it to me," said Lynn. Quite clearly, when it came to rules and regulations these Maidenhead Static Model Club guys did not mess around. After a bit of cajoling he did take it in the end and I know Lynn and I did have a laugh about it afterwards. Even so, at every Windsor fair after that, I was always up to re-book before the clock turned three.

Whilst Windsor was the fair for diecast, Gloucester was definitely the place for trains. The doors to the hall would open at 8am with some traders arriving from as early as 6am to claim the best of the parking spots and, just like Windsor, this was also the time for many to conduct a little early business. All manner of goodies would be set out on top of car bonnets, or on show in open car boots. It was great fun just walking around the car park and checking out what was on offer.

One particular Saturday, a television crew had arrived at Gloucester. They were making a programme based on a day in the life of a dealer, and the person under the spotlight was Ken Simmons. The crew began recording him as he was getting his stock together at home in Bristol and they travelled with him as he made his way to Gloucester. Once he had parked up, they were filming as he walked around the car park looking at the goods on display. Roger Mazillius, the man who started Vectis Auctions, had arrived early as usual and was parked up with some toys laid out for sale.

I am not sure exactly what it was of Roger's that had caught Ken's eye, but with the cameras whirring he asked Roger the price. "It's a hundred and ten pounds Ken, but

Ken Simmons with space toy

you can have it for a hundred," said Roger. After another examination, Ken decided that, yes he would buy it and on the car bonnet carefully counted out one hundred pounds in ten pound notes. Roger, fully aware that the camera was capturing his every move and wanting to show that he was doing everything correctly, picked up the money, held it in the air and in a loud, measured voice said "Thank you, Ken. I'll bank that first thing on Monday."

Once the unloading doors were open at Gloucester, the thrill was looking round as the tables were being set up. Always exciting would be to come across someone who was pulling out rare items, or others that might be a little on the cheap side. Any table with items like this could generate a buying frenzy, which quickly became infectious. In no time at all a crowd maybe three or four deep would gather round, with everyone wanting to be in on the act, trying to grab what was on offer. Buying decisions had to be made quickly. If you hesitated for a second, you knew someone behind would be waiting to pounce.

Gradually, as the cheaper items were snapped up, the crowd would thin. Still at the table though would be all the late-comers, those people who had missed the real bargains, but who were nevertheless determined to get something from the place where all the action had been, the place they were sure must be good to buy from. Every remaining item on the table would be examined for some merit, however small, and perfectly sane people would end up parting with good money for toys or trains they would never have considered in more rational circumstances. In truth, any one of us in a situation like that could easily be carried away by the moment and become guilty of paying prices that, on any other day, we would be happy to sell at.

In this frantic environment, there was nothing quite as potent as someone that nobody knew turning up – a fresh unrecognised face behind the table to kick-start this hysteria. Once you became a regular stallholder, it was never quite the same. As soon as certain people saw it was me or any of the Gloucester regulars standing there, it did not matter how attractive our prices might have been; because we were known to be dealers, psychologically, they felt they were wasting their time looking for bargains. There is no doubt in my mind that those tables manned by stallholders they knew – the very ones they normally walked straight past without a second glance – would have been viewed as places to buy from if only someone they did not recognise had been standing there.

In some of my wilder moments, I imagined one day getting a friend, whom no one had seen before, to book a table. It would be in his name and I would equip him with a whole pile of my stock to sell. Someone completely out of the blue arriving with a table full of goodies – it would be irresistible. I visualised him unpacking a few cheap pieces to begin with to get people's attention. Then, with everyone crowding around and all feeling that this has to be the place to buy from, it would only need the prices to be a fraction lower than normal for things to be sailing away. I am convinced that the whole table would have been cleared hook line and sinker and for the same money I would have been very happy to take myself. I really don't have much to sell now so it is too late, but I wish I had done it back then just to prove the point.

Gloucester in its heyday was awash with activity, interest and excitement. The venue had one major drawback, however. The lighting inside was not only of a fairly low level but it embellished everything in the hall with a sort of orange tint. The original colours of trains in particular were distorted and very often someone would ask if they could take whatever they were considering buying to one of the unloading doors, to examine it in daylight. This was never a problem with regular Gloucester visitors, but with any unfamiliar face it was always something I was slightly apprehensive about. There was always a slight concern just in case the man should open the door then suddenly race off down the road clutching a prime piece of Hornby. Fortunately, it never happened.

One day late in 1979, there was even an auction of trains at Gloucester. In the side annexe, Tim Armitage personally conducted a sale of 90 lots, of which, according to the Collectors Gazette, 75 were sold. I remember the auction and in particular a Bing for Bassett-Lowke live steam 'County of Northampton', stripped of paint and minus its tender, selling for £400. The Collectors Gazette quotes Tim as saying "It was a good idea and I'd like to run another as it added extra interest to the event." It cannot have been too long after this that extra stalls filled that side annexe, so that could have been the reason why no more auctions took place.

When I was buying and selling trains, my table at Gloucester was against the wall next to Mike and Shelia Brown's. Marie and I would travel down, sometimes with the boys as well, which was good as it meant that there were plenty of us to keep an eye on things and take turns to look around. I always liked to have a wander round the stalls early on and of course that was also the best time to sell.

Anyone who deals in collectables at fairs faces the same dilemma – do you look round and do some buying first thing, or stay at the table and try to sell when everyone is red hot to buy? With me it was always the looking round that won through, and so, before coming down, Marie would insist on everything being

Tim Armitage (left) displaying some of his early models and
Michael Foster with his newly produced trains

priced if she was to be looking after the table. Inevitably of course it was not, and
after her continually having to say "I'm not sure" to price enquirers, I would always
promise to get it right the next time.

On one occasion during the week leading up to Gloucester I took a telephone call
from a man in the Kings Heath area of Birmingham. He told me that he had a
clockwork tramcar made by Märklin and he was thinking of selling it. The tramcar
had been bought by his grandfather from the Birmingham shop Walker and
Holtzapffel (not surprisingly later abbreviated to W & H) in 1913. I was more
familiar at that time with Hornby and Bassett-Lowke trains than tramcars. Vaguely
aware, however, that anything by Märklin was good news, I drove over to his house
to see it.

The tram was hand painted, maybe ten inches long, with a hinged roof and seating
with spikes, which would once have held composition figures in place. A long key

through the roof wound the clockwork mechanism underneath and it had a clever geared linkage through to one of the two 4-wheeled bogies. I asked him how much he wanted, expecting one of the usual responses in such situations, which would either be that he hadn't a clue, an invitation for me to make an offer, or a combination of the two. Instead, he surprised me by immediately declaring he wanted £100. The price seemed right enough and I paid him the money.

Years later, by chance, I happened to find out that the valuation at that figure and the identification as Märklin was information given to him by a collector friend of mine, Ted Doyle, when he was shown the tramcar during an exhibition of trains at Stoneleigh. The Birmingham gentleman had declined to sell at the time and, after showing the piece to Ted, took it back home.

I felt happy that the tramcar was a good buy at £100. As to whether it was worth much more, I wasn't sure, but I knew someone who would almost certainly know. Mike Brown had an interest in the German makes such as Bing, Carette and Märklin. As Gloucester was coming up at the weekend and we would be next to each other as usual, he was the obvious person to show it to. Behind the table at Gloucester, Mike studied the piece and came to the conclusion that it had to be worth three or four hundred pounds if it was worth a penny, which was very pleasing. I hadn't brought it down with the intention of selling, so I placed it behind a bookshelf at the back of the table for safekeeping, whilst I wandered around the fair as usual.

Gloucester attracted quite a few European buyers at the time and when I returned to the table, Marie told me that a Dutchman had spotted the tramcar and wanted to know the price. She had told him that it was not for sale but, undeterred, he declared his intention to return to see me, which he did whilst Marie and I were stood there talking. I explained to him that I had only brought the piece down to show my friend, to which he replied "Look, I make you an offer," (in Dutch English of course). I told him that he could make me an offer if he wanted to, but it would make no difference; it still wouldn't be for sale. "I give you nine hundred pounds," he went on to say, for which I thanked him, told him I would think about it and placed it back behind the bookshelf.

Allen Levy, at the time, was actively searching out toys for his new museum in London, and earlier in the day he had asked me to put a couple of items aside. When he returned to pick them up, and just as he was getting his chequebook out to settle, he spied the Märklin piece. "How much is the re-painted tramcar?" I told him that it was not re-painted and neither was it for sale. His response, which I will always treasure as an illustration of Allen's undoubted negotiating skill, was "How much would it be if it was for sale?" I considered that question for a few seconds. Bearing

David Burt, Joan Dunk, Marie, Graham de Chastelain and Peter Dunk at our house in 2003

in mind the offer of nine hundred and mindful of all this apparent interest, I quickly came to the view that perhaps I wasn't too bothered about holding onto it after all. I looked at Allen and casually answered "Twelve hundred." Quick as a flash, to close the deal, he said, "I'll take it," and I said, "OK."

Not half an hour had passed, before I believe it was first Tim Armitage and then John Haley and then David Burt who came over to see me. None of them seemed best pleased that I had failed to show the tramcar to them first.

In my experience, if something has been sold cheaply with no possible chance of recovery, interested observers then tend to jump in with suggested valuations, always sky high as if to accentuate just how low the price had been in the first place.

Irving Brim with his Triang Minics and trains

This case was no different and estimates from two thousand pounds upward were proffered, until someone said "It could be worth ten grand." This might have been a touch fanciful, but, as I learnt very clearly that day, certain Märklin items could be in a league of their own.

It might sound strange to some people, but what I used to enjoy as much as anything in these situations was simply the buzz of doing the deal – the buying and selling. Looking back now, I would rather have the memory of that incident working out the way it did, than still owning that tramcar and thinking it must be worth whatever. In fact, I remember Allen and I having a laugh about it afterwards – or was it just him that was laughing now I come to think of it? Anyway, at least it gave me something to bank first thing on Monday.

Exotic items like Märklin tramcars, which would turn up once in a blue moon, were all well and good, but as far as my buying and selling were concerned, 0 gauge trains, in particular Hornby and Bassett-Lowke, were the things I was into. I placed 'Wanted' ads in the magazines, but probably most productive for me during the 1980s were the auction houses in London.

Unlike today, auctions for toys and trains at that time were not as popular with collectors. Descriptions were often vague and, unless you took the trouble to view, you could not always be certain of what you were buying, which was not entirely conducive to absentee bidding. In those days, by attending these auctions regularly, I had some very good buys.

Despite the sales at Christies, Sotheby's and Phillips all being in central London, I always preferred to drive down, rather than take the train. Parking was not straightforward, but I would get to know precisely where all the parking meters in the area were and I enjoyed the convenience of the car. It also gave me the advantage of being able to buy any of the bigger and bulkier lots in the sales. These were the ones unable to be considered by people travelling there by public transport, and very often those yielding more profit. At that time I had a succession of Citroën CX estate cars; vehicles which could hold an awful lot of trains.

There were occasional auctions for toys outside of London. Sotheby's in Chester was one. Another was Phillips in Knowle (now Bonhams) and decent collections would be sold there from time to time. It was also much nearer and more convenient

Colin Walker with his diecast models

Ellis and a very large bus

for me than central London. My younger son Ellis was at one time very interested in Hornby Dublo. So much so, that he sold it mainly through a mail order list. It was at a sale in Knowle that he bought one very large lot of Hornby Dublo which included a couple of heavy boxed controllers.

Controllers are not things you would normally take much notice of, just as he didn't. The weight of each of the boxes felt about the same, although the contents turned out to be a little different. Opening them back home, perhaps as long as a month after the sale, whilst one contained what was expected, tightly fitted inside the other were two Bing for Bassett-Lowke 0 gauge '112' Tank locomotives in very nice condition. The box had clearly never been opened after being consigned for auction.

My own sales list was largely of 0 gauge trains, with a smattering of gauge 1. The list was sent mostly to customers overseas, for two very good reasons. Firstly, many collectors in Australia and New Zealand were very keen on Hornby, just as they are now. I had a string of good customers down under for many years and apart from the odd one getting confused over the time zones and telephoning to ask about a particular Hornby train at three o'clock in the morning, they were invariably nice people to deal with. Unfortunately, for many of them, their buying activities began to falter once prices over here started to rise substantially and the Australian dollar began to fall heavily against the pound.

The second reason I chose to sell abroad was purely financial – there was no VAT to account for on exported goods. Unlike the current position, where a trader's VAT liability can be restricted to apply to the profit margin only, in the early 1980s the tax was payable on the total amount the goods were sold for, regardless of the cost price. Having to pay the government a blanket 15% (as it was then) on the full selling price of everything sold in the UK was a ludicrous state of affairs and unless you were someone operating on huge profit margins (no example names suggested), was completely unworkable.

Dealing in second-hand goods rather than new meant that VAT could not be claimed back on the vast majority of stock purchased. That in itself was bad enough, but buying say a train for £100 and selling it to someone in the UK for £110 would have meant paying the government around £15 in VAT and finishing up by losing a fiver on the transaction. That is why I was doing my bit for the export drive.

Once the list went out, after a few days the phone would be red hot with orders and pretty soon the cheques would start arriving, all of which was great. The only element in all of this to really spoil the party was packing the parcels. Trains and especially large railway accessories like stations and engine sheds all finished up as massive parcels and were the devil's own job to pack. Buyers would pay the postage costs, which was just as well, as to places like Australia and New Zealand air freight could often be £70 or more a time.

The counter staff at the Market Harborough Post Office got to know me very well, and it would be a safe bet to assume that I was not their favourite customer. Arriving at the counter with perhaps ten or twenty massive overseas parcels to send, I could see their faces visibly drop. For them, processing these awkward bulky packages must have been much more of a chore than dishing out stamps or pension money.

For Marie and I though, after hours of packing these trains, it was great to be rid of them and to have the house, which had been swamped with cardboard boxes, bubble wrap, tissue paper and parcel tape for the past week, back to normal. We would be clear of the mess, only until it was time for the next list. I realise now that if I had been dealing in something like Dinky Toys, which are tiny when compared with trains, the parcel side of things would have been a doddle. I have always been a train man, but if ever I were to start another mail order business, it seems to me that buying and selling diecast toys would be a whole lot easier.

I did not have all that many customers in the USA. Most people over there naturally wanted American outline trains, although there were a few exceptions and one particular man would call me every three or four days simply to see what I had newly acquired in the Hornby line. This went on for about two or three years and he would take almost everything I had that was hard to find or simply in nice condition. One day, he phoned to say that he had a project urgently requiring finance and the collection had to be sold right away, just like that. As he had always bought the most desirable trains, the very things a queue of people a mile long would want, it did not take the two of us long to agree a price. He arranged to airfreight the collection over and I emptied the trailer van we used for transporting trestle tables to the fairs.

Within three weeks of his call, I was driving back from Heathrow with the trailer van packed tight with thirty to forty very large boxes, each crammed full of pre-war Hornby trains. As luck would have it, Hornby prices, especially for the quality items he had been buying, had shot up in the few years since his collecting had begun. This, coupled with the dollar dropping back against the pound, meant that I was able to pay him a good price and buy a cracking collection I could sell like falling off a log. It was a little strange opening the boxes and seeing again all those trains we had carefully wrapped up and mailed out over the past few years, now back again once more.

It was abundantly clear to me that, instead of mailing all these trains out to him in perhaps sixty or more parcels over that period, it would have been far less trouble for me to have kept the lot and simply sold them three years later when prices were so much higher. That would have been too easy though, and after all, who else was going to keep those Post Office staff employed?

A DEALER'S LIFE FOR ME

9

It's great to buy

Buying was always the most enjoyable part for me, and one particular collection took me over to Jersey. I took a call from a man whose father had recently died and the family needed to dispose of their Bassett-Lowke 0 gauge railway. Speaking on the telephone, he gave me a rough idea of what was there and it sounded good, but I also had the impression that I might not have been the only person he was calling, which meant I needed to act quickly if I was going to buy.

To reach the Channel Islands by car and ferry would have been a long haul just on the off chance that I might have bought the collection, so I decided that the best option was to fly over. This was going to be the quickest and easiest way to get there. Obviously I would be unable to bring it back with me, but at least I could try and secure a deal. I located a day return flight from the East Midlands airport to Jersey for £75 and called the man there to expect me.

He picked me up from the airport in St. Helier and drove me to his house where I was introduced to his mother and brother. The family had moved to Jersey only a year or so earlier from Scotland, where they had lived in some style in a large country house with the trains running outside. They told me that the railway had run for fully half a mile on their Scottish estate and when I saw the loose trackwork piled up outside their home in Jersey, I could well believe it. The railway had been dismantled and brought over to Jersey, where the father had fully intended to rebuild it, albeit in a smaller way. Shortly after the move from Scotland, however, he was taken ill and had sadly died before any track laying could begin.

The locomotives were almost all Bassett-Lowke. Amongst others were two streamlined A4s, six 'Duchess' class, four examples of 'Flying Scotsman', six Compounds, six 0-6-0 tender locomotives, six 0-6-0 tanks, a 'Deltic' diesel, a Märklin 2-6-4 tank and a very large streamlined American outline locomotive in brass. There were quite a few wagons and no less than 120 Exley coaches. The owner had obviously been a fan of Scottish railways, for almost every single item including the 120 Exley coaches, had been re-painted in Highland Railway green. There were also some accessories and, of course, the half a mile of track.

We managed to agree a price for the collection. The price covered everything bar the track, as there was no way I could bring that back easily. Luckily, one of the sons had been in touch with a model railway group on the island who had already expressed an interest in the track, so that particular problem appeared to be solved. Everything else, I calculated, should just about fit into my Volkswagen Passat with the back seats down. We shook hands and I agreed to come back with my car a week or so later.

Coming over on the ferry from Portsmouth to Jersey was a long journey and I booked hotel accommodation for a couple of nights on the island in order to take in a little sightseeing, before meeting up with the train family again. Peering into an antiques shop window in St. Helier, I spotted a Triang Minic clockwork lorry with the very rare 'Brockhouse' trailer. It was the first one I had ever seen and at £22 it was decidedly more than a good buy and one of the very few occasions I have found anything in the toy line worth buying from an antiques shop. I later swapped the piece with a friend, Eric Cato, for a couple of minor toys and an oil painting he had always understood to be of somewhere in Northern France. I recognised the scene right away, however, as Staithes on the Yorkshire coast and, after re-framing, the picture now hangs on a wall at home.

Back in Jersey, before packing the trains, the family kindly showed me some cine film of the railway running in Scotland. Shot during the 1950s, the scenes showed trains belting along the half a mile of track. Sat there watching these films and reliving memories of their garden railway, what provided the family with the most amusement (although it was somewhat less amusing to me) were the staged crashes. I looked on in disbelief as time and time again one train was deliberately driven into another resulting in everything then flying up in the air. After witnessing all this carnage in miniature, I could understand much better why everything in the collection had been re-painted. When it was time to go, we only just managed to cram everything into the Passat. I didn't want to leave anything behind, so every inch of space in that car was utilised.

Getting back to England was not so straightforward. This would have been February or March time and, due to extremely rough sea conditions, the return ferry had been cancelled and I had no choice other than to stay another night in Jersey. Even the next day the weather seemed just as bad and it was touch and go whether the ferry would be delayed again, until the decision was made at the last moment to sail. I had never considered myself a particularly bad sailor, but that trip back from Jersey was horrendous. The sailing time was about nine hours, although a lifetime seemed more accurate. Waves were crashing against the windows, the ship was lurching in all directions and every passenger was sat not uttering a word, just waiting for the ordeal to be over. It sounds a bit soft to say this about a regular ferry journey, but I can remember wondering whether we really would make it back. Had we not done so, then I dare say someone would eventually have passed comment on my at least managing to take the trains with me.

Driving through customs was not much of a concern. The way the trains were packed in the car with bits sticking out here there and everywhere, it looked more like a load of scrap rather than anything that could possibly attract duty. I told the Customs officer it was old model railway stuff and as he probably didn't fancy delving into it anyway, he just waved me through.

One of the A4s from Jersey now belongs to the professional restorer Chris Littledale and can be seen on page 30 of the 'Collectors' Guide to Toy Trains' by Ron McCrindell, completely dismantled and stripped of paint ready for restoration. Two of the 'Flying Scotsman' locomotives from the collection, although most definitely made by Bassett-Lowke, were unusual in being entirely of brass construction and the only ones I have ever seen built in that way. One of them, still in its Highland Railway green, turned up in a Rugby auction only a few years ago.

Whilst my 'Wanted' ads for trains were quite successful, very often someone visiting one of the fairs would have a collection to sell. I remember being at the Birmingham Clarendon Suite one evening when a man told me of his late father's collection of Hornby and other 0 gauge trains. Attempting to give me an idea of what was there, he could recall the locomotives and coaches clearly enough and he knew there were plenty of wagons, although the only one he could bring to mind by name was a 'Crawford's Biscuits' van. It sounded a collection worth going to see

The Jersey collection locomotives

and I made arrangements to meet him a few days later at his garage business near to Wolverhampton.

On arrival, I could see the trains all nicely laid out in one corner of the workshop. There were indeed some nice items – two or three locomotives, coaches and many accessories including a Carette for Bassett-Lowke 'Four Oaks' English Station. A pleasant surprise was that his father must have been a collector, rather than just someone whose trains had survived from childhood. This had to be the case, for there was an example of almost every Hornby private owner van, right from the early 1920s 'Colman's Mustard' and 'Seccotine' to the late 1930s 'Palethorpes'. All of them were unboxed, but every one was in very nice condition. The only van which was not there was the very one he had remembered earlier. I could understand though how the name had stuck in his mind. In the whole of the collection there was just one solitary original box. Nothing whatever inside, but the label read 'Crawford's Biscuits'.

Forever dealing in trains meant that I didn't focus too much on the diecast side, unless a batch of Dinky, Corgi or similar toys happened to come along without too much trouble somewhere or other. It was during the early 1980s that a train collector friend introduced me to someone very keen on acquiring gauge 1 trains. I happened to have a lot of them spare at the time, although the man concerned didn't have any money, which on the face of it would not usually have been a good combination.

All, however, was not lost, as he was keen to draw my attention to the diecast he had for swaps. Whenever I had bought Dinky or other diecast in the past, it had generally sold well. Not specialising in it meant that my prices were probably on the low side, which of course is more than helpful it comes to selling. I was keen, therefore, to find out what he had to swap and arranged to call and see him, taking everything I had available in the gauge 1 line along with me. This included three or four fairly impressive Bing for Bassett-Lowke locomotives, including an Atlantic and a 'George the Fifth', some coaches and quite a few of the Carette for Bassett–Lowke wagons.

As soon as I had arrived and before I could get any trains unpacked, he wanted to show me what was up in the loft. The whole roof area was simply crammed with diecast – boxed, unboxed, Dinky, Corgi, Spot-On, Matchbox, everything seemed to be there. There was so much to look at and as I wasn't sure exactly which models he was prepared to swap, or indeed whether he wanted any of my trains anyway, I suggested that he take a look at the gauge 1 first and we could proceed from there.

His own gauge 1 collection consisted mainly of a few small tank engines, and the minute he caught sight of the large locomotives I had, he wanted them all. Fortunately, this meant that we could dispense with the need to discuss anything so vulgar as prices, as he simply asked right away if I would take the loft full of diecast as a straight swap. I wasn't too familiar with diecast values, but it seemed to me that, with the number of items I had seen lying in that roof space, on this occasion I had no need to be. It wouldn't have taken Einstein to figure out that there would have been more chance of flying to the moon than this being an unfavourable swap and I had no hesitation in agreeing to it.

Strangely enough, even though I knew the swap was a good one, I remember being equally pleased to find someone as keen as I was becoming on gauge 1. Even though I was collecting the stuff myself, it never seemed as though too many others were doing the same, which always puzzled me. There are perhaps a few more collectors of gauge 1 about now, but back then everyone seemed to prefer the smaller trains. Although this man had been a collector of various toys and trains for many years, it was the first time he had seen any of these bigger locomotives in the flesh and it was great to see his new-found enthusiasm. He had not looked at the diecast for years, but in getting these large gauge 1 engines, his collecting had suddenly acquired a new lease of life.

All that remained was to get the diecast down from the loft and pack my car. He climbed up into the rafters to pass things down through the loft hatch, whilst I started to fill my Citroën CX Estate. The annoying thing was, I couldn't fit everything in. I was already well versed on buying trips to filling every conceivable inch of space in that car. In fact on every previous occasion after buying a large collection, I had always managed to find room somewhere for every single toy or train, sometimes against seemingly impossible odds. This time, however, even with my whale of a vehicle, defeat had to be admitted. I remember having to leave behind a whole pile of boxed Matchbox cars and among other things what I later recognised to be a pre-war Dinky Toy Petrol Station.

It was great fun sorting through all the goodies at home the next day, but as I wasn't an expert on diecast, I called a friend of mine who was. Roy Laycock came down from Sheffield and took a lot of the Dinky and Spot-On models. He didn't want the Matchbox Yesteryears (nothing changes) and I must have sold the early first series models sometime later, but amongst the collection was a very large tray full of the Matchbox veteran style cars all unboxed.

The Market Harborough evening fair was coming up and I had decided to take the Yesteryear cars along. They were still sitting in the tray when I wrote on a large piece of card 'All £2 each.' Andrew Clark was round first and carefully picked out a dozen or maybe more. I never really had Andrew marked down as someone into Yesteryear cars and when I asked him about this he said "No, but these are all preproduction samples." You have to know your diecast. Unless of course there is a loft full of it – and then what does it matter?

I believe it was getting this diecast collection that inspired my eldest son Simon to become interested. He began collecting Dinky Toys and was very soon into buying and selling diecast, especially models in top condition. For a while he even rented a stand in Leicester Antiques Centre, which was fairly good, but as he was not there too often himself and could not always depend on the Antiques Centre staff to look after the customers, business was patchy. Simon preferred to sell at the fairs, where he was in charge. He always had a good eye for condition. Indeed, only recently, John Martin was reminding me of the many mint and boxed pieces he bought from Simon years ago.

Most of my own buying and selling was in trains. This was mainly during the 1980s when prices seemed to be rising by leaps and bounds. The reason for this can only have been due to a generation of younger people, myself included (we were all young once), all becoming interested around the same time. With so many of us out and about looking for these toys and trains during that same period, values could only ever have gone one way.

This hike in prices often went on much to the amazement of the older generation of collectors. For some of them, after a while their objective in coming to a fair or anywhere toys or trains might be on sale began to change. It soon became not a case of seeing what might be there to buy, but an opportunity to re-assess the value of their collection. If you had something on a sales table without a price ticket, their question would be "How much are these worth nowadays, just out of interest?" or "How much would one of these be worth – just the same as yours but with a green roof?" Suddenly, everything these older collectors had picked up years ago, at prices we 'new kids on the block' would have considered next to nothing, was now worth serious money. It wasn't only collectors who were surprised at the prices. In those days, whenever anyone with no interest in collecting just walked off the street into a fair, one glance at the price of all this stuff they once had as kids, especially diecast, and they would stand back in amazement "I've got all these at home – all better than this. I must be sitting on a fortune," or "Just look at these prices. I threw all mine out years ago – I should have kept them."

The strange thing is, you hardly ever hear those comments now. What with a constant stream of TV programmes such as Antiques Roadshow, Cash in the Attic, Bargain Hunt and Flog it, all telling us what this is worth or what that is worth, the situation today has changed completely. Nowadays, rather than being surprised that something from their childhood might have some value, unless they have been stuck in outer Mongolia for the past fifteen years, every person in the land will just assume it has.

10

A right royal provenance

Any overview of the toy collecting scene over the past thirty years would not be complete without the mention of one particular name. I realise that any reference to Jeffrey Levitt might raise a few eyebrows in some quarters, but he was so very much a part of the toy scene during the 1980s, and as such cannot be ignored.

Jeffrey Levitt, I believe, began his toy collecting with Dinky Toys. My first recollection of him was at a toy fair organised by Colin and Sarah Baddiel at the Ivanhoe Hotel in London. It was there that I remember him buying from me a Dinky Toy 'Capstan' van. He went on to cultivate a mail order business in Dinky Toys and it was his success in this area that motivated him to go much further in the toy collecting business. He founded his company Mint & Boxed in the early 1980s, opening first a shop in Hendon and then larger and more prestigious premises, sporting an upstairs showroom and boardroom, in Edgware.

He was buying collections all the while, paying top prices and producing regular, elaborate, full colour catalogues to showcase his sales stock. From his original base of diecast models, he quickly spread his buying net to pull in no end of quality tinplate toys and trains. One of his best-known purchases was the complete tin toy car collection belonging to the Swiss dealer and collector Peter Ottenheimer, after it had been the subject of the book Toy Autos 1890-1939.

Advertising and a strong image were important for Jeffrey Levitt's business and the Mint & Boxed full colour magazine ads were photographic works of art, which must have been welcomed with open arms by the financial departments of all the various collecting publications. It was the Mint & Boxed ads in fact which first brought colour to the Collectors Gazette, where they occupied full centre spread from the mid 1980s until the very early 1990s.

It was a widely held belief among all of us on the toy scene at the time that Jeffrey Levitt had inherited a family fortune and that, in building this high profile business, he was doing no more than indulging his passion. At first, the amount of money left to him was rumoured to be a couple of million pounds and, as the Mint & Boxed operation expanded, so the perceived inheritance figure grew, until it was reckoned that forty million might be nearer the mark. Jeffrey Levitt was forever to be seen in magazines and even the financial papers, in his endeavours to elevate toy collecting to the same level as fine art and have people regard toys as a good investment.

The Mint & Boxed shop was an Aladdin's cave of fabulous toys and was managed at one time by Dick Tout, a large and very friendly man. Whenever I, or probably anyone he knew walked through the door, Jeffrey was always keen to convey the impression of big business being done all the while and would shout things like "Dick! Make sure you get those Cadillacs off to Tokyo." I think it was Colin Baddiel who, in voicing his opinion, talked in terms of "Orchestrated Bullshit", which was perhaps appropriate.

I was in the shop one day when Jeffrey showed me a very early Märklin gauge 1 train set, comprising a locomotive, tender and two coaches. It was accompanied by a framed photograph of the Tsar of Russia and his young son, pictured with the very same train set on a side table. I remember commenting to Jeffrey on the train's incredible provenance and telling him that I thought his price of £30,000 not out of the way. The next time I saw the train was when Jeffrey Levitt had it with him during an appearance on breakfast television. He was expounding the virtues of buying toys and with very good reason, for the price of that particular Märklin set, in the year or so since I had examined it, had risen more than five times to no less than £169,000. Now – who says these trains are not a good investment?

Perhaps Jeffrey Levitt's biggest move was the setting up of a gallery in New York. The opening party was a very glitzy affair, attracting celebrities such as Brooke Shields and Richard Gere. Money was being spent freely, but what did it matter – Jeffrey was a rich man and was enjoying himself. Even though many would shake their heads at some of Mint & Boxed's incredibly high prices, there was a distinct feeling among many others that he was bringing new collectors into the hobby and taking the whole toy collecting scene to a new level. It was a heady time. Everything then seemed positive and on the up and we were all being swept along on a wave of optimism.

When the bubble did finally burst in 1991, the news came as a bolt out of the blue to everyone. It was hard to believe that there had been no inheritance after all, just unpaid debts amounting to millions of pounds. With audacious nerve, Jeffrey Levitt had managed to persuade various high street banks and even a former Lord Mayor of London to advance him many millions of pounds against the security of false sales figures and accounts. He had even been awarded the Queen's Award for Export Achievement, based presumably on the very same figures. He was eventually sentenced to four years imprisonment for fraud and paroled after serving two years of his sentence.

As part of the liquidation of the Mint & Boxed assets, an auction of the remaining stock from the company was held at Sotheby's. Among a saleroom full of all manner of diecast models, tin toys and trains coming up for sale, one particular lot caught my eye. It was none other than the Tsar's train. With it of course was the photograph of the Tsar with the train. But also included now were many other photos – some of the Tsar without the train, others of the train without the Tsar and so on. The image of the train set had been cleverly superimposed onto an old photograph of the Russian leader and his son. The train's illustrious provenance, the very thing to confer unique value upon it, had been no more than an elaborate scam. Even though its provenance was bogus, the train was still a nice early Märklin set and sold in the auction for around £17,000.

About ten years later, the train set came under the hammer for a second time (mine in fact) at Rugby, when it was knocked down for £22,000. There is no doubt whatsoever that even though no member of the Royal House of Romanov ever laid eyes on it, that Märklin set will always occupy its own special place in toy collecting folklore and will forever be known as 'The Tsar's Train'.

If there was ever to be a published list of the most popular phrases associated with collectable items being offered for sale, there is one that would have to be somewhere near to the top. After having a toy or train offered to you on the telephone and you feel the need to enquire about its condition, the classic response is "It's in good condition for its age". What does this mean? Does anyone out there really know? After thirty odd years of messing about with these things, I for one have still to find out. The reality, of course, is that it can mean anything the seller wants it to. In my experience, after seeing more than a few things described in this way, there is no doubt that to some people it must mean that the item in question has survived – but only just.

I would take a bet though, that there is one place where this 'suggest everything and promise nothing' description would be very much at home. It is a place where from what I have heard, the blind are very often leading the blind. I don't buy or sell anything on the internet myself, but I can imagine it being a very familiar phrase to those who do.

In fact, when some of these internet guys really want to go to town and have absolutely nothing left to chance, they may not be content with anything so understated as simply 'Good condition for its age'. Someone told me recently that he spotted a much more bullish and uncompromising statement on the electronic market place – namely 'Mint condition for its age'. Never mind the toys and trains – they won't change much from how they look now – but wouldn't it be a lovely world, if as the years pass by and we all grow old gracefully, we could still apply that particular description to ourselves?

With the advent of the internet revolution that many people now take for granted, it is easy to forget what a recent phenomenon this has been. I first began to take notice of it as recently as May 1999, when Marie and I were on holiday in the USA. I remember being amazed by the number of company names shown on billboards and in television ads which had .com at the end of them, when such things were almost unheard of over here. Buying and selling on-line has become a way of life for some people, and good luck to them.

What amuses me about it all is hearing of a trader, whom many of us out here in the 'non cyberspace world' have known for ages as someone to be a bit wary of, suddenly being acclaimed on the internet as the best thing since sliced bread. A 'top seller', or 'a dealer you can trust'. It seems to matter not what you have been up to in the past, you can go on-line, the slate will be immediately wiped clean and everything will be absolutely great.

The horror stories you hear are hardly surprising. The fact is that when you are buying from someone whose only interest is doing whatever it takes, no holds barred, to get as much money as possible for something they know absolutely nothing about, it is hard to imagine any better recipe for disaster. If as a seller, a few deals go wrong and people start complaining that things you have sold are not as described, that's no real problem – blow them, you can simply disappear from that arena, take out a new identity and start all over again. What could be easier? For all those unlucky people tempted to deal with you, however, it brings the phrase 'Buyer Beware' into very sharp focus.

After saying that, I am sure that buying on the internet can be perfectly safe, good fun and productive, provided that you know plenty about what it is you are buying and you are careful over whom you buy from. The problem lies not with the established dealers, the ones who have a reputation to look after, the ones who want you to be satisfied so that you will come back time and time again. The real difficulty with buying on-line it seems to me is the lack of regulation, the fact that so few people can be held accountable. Because companies such as e-bay adopt a policy of only limited responsibility, if any, when it comes to the authenticity of items or accuracy of descriptions, the hardest thing I suspect is sorting out the wheat from the chaff.

I dare say as time goes by things will improve as they must, because feeling comfortable about buying anything without first seeing the item is all about having confidence in the seller. I know that with e-bay there is a facility for the buyer to leave a comment after making a purchase, but this is not always meaningful, as very often the buyer does not want to be critical for fear of any negative feedback being reciprocated. I feel sure that in time the whole thing will be regulated more firmly, and buying on line will be less hazardous. Even then, I am sure that we traditional stick-in-the-muds who prefer to buy and sell things the established way by talking to a real person and actually being able to see something before we buy it, will still be doing things our way.

As mentioned earlier, right from the days when I was simply collecting I placed regular ads in the 'Wanted' columns of train magazines like the Railway Modeller. The response to these was generally good, although not every reply was a piece of cake to deal with. There was always a little eager anticipation waiting to see what was described, especially whenever anyone called mentioning trains that had been in the family since pre-war days, perhaps ones belonging to a father or grandfather.

Unfortunately, there are times when any of us can get a little confused and forget just how long, or maybe how not so long, things have been around for. I remember on a few occasions speaking to such a caller and after asking for more details of the engines, like how many wheels or what numbers are visible on the side, they would mention the British Railways lettering. After your heart dropped, you then had to tell them that it could not be pre-war with that lettering, as British Railways did not exist until 1948. You had to say that you were very sorry, but they must be mistaken. I have known the caller then get quite angry and start to argue that it definitely was, it belonged to their granddad for goodness sake. I distinctly remember one person say "There's no doubt about it – are you calling me a liar?"

Let's face it. At the end of the day most of us want as peaceful and as carefree a life as possible, so once this has happened a couple of times and exactly the same scenario begins to unfold again, you learn to just go with the flow. You have to agree with what is being said and simply accept the fact that they have the only pre-war British Railways Hornby engine in the world.

Unlike me, some people are naturally well organised and like to confront any situation fully prepared. Very commendable of course, although sometimes the preparation can be a little overdone. Like, for example, the person who would call about trains they had for sale and be sat there ready on the end of the line, with a list describing every item in meticulous detail. After the initial pleasantries, all they are really waiting for is your question "What have you got?" This is their cue to give you the works. All well meaning of course, but it is then simply impossible to halt the presentation until every item has been mentioned in triplicate.

First, they will tell you about each engine, the number on its side, the number on the box, everything. The same rigorous detail then is recited for every single wagon and every single coach. At that point, just when you think – I have got the whole picture, there can be nothing more in the world I need to know about this person's trains – that is when they will start on the track. "Sixteen straights, fifteen curves." You jump in to say, "Don't worry about the track." "Fourteen half straights, three left-hand points" "No, look! It really doesn't matter about the track." "Four right-hand points, three quarter curves," and so on. That list has been prepared and you are not going anywhere until you have been told all there is to know about every single item on it.

The hardest track of all to sell was always tinplate Hornby 0 gauge clockwork in poor condition and I had piles of it. One day, after this stuff had been cluttering up my garage forever and a day, I decided that the only sensible place for it was the tip. It completely filled my car, but in one fell swoop I was rid of the lot. As it happened, the very next day a man called, telling me that he had seen my 'Wanted' advert and had some train stuff to sell. After asking him for details, he explained that he didn't actually have any engines or even any rolling stock for that matter. In fact, all that he had was track, but there was plenty of it.

Apparently he had been lucky and had managed to get hold of it only the day before. He told me that he knew this old train stuff was worth good money, but that I could have it at a fair price. The best thing of all, he told me, was that he was local. In fact just down the road and he could even bring it over to show me. I thanked him for the offer and politely told him that it sounded nice, but I was absolutely fine on the track front. Tempting as it was, I just didn't have the heart to say any more.

A DEALER'S LIFE FOR ME

11

Over the water

I have never been a regular visitor to fairs abroad. I have, however, enjoyed a few visits to the Toymania show in Paris and trips to the huge fleamarket to the north of the city at Porte de Cligancourt. Walking around the fleamarket, where maybe a dozen toy dealers had permanent booths, was great, and I used to buy a lot of French Hornby from there, sometimes taking over English trains to swap. As well as the trains, it was tin cars that I used to look out for most in Paris, ones like the large 1920s and 1930s Citroën models that I was collecting at the time.

I remember just beating one of the French dealers at Toymania to a boxed Citroën car. I cannot recall the particular model, but I know it was one I was keen to get and

Roy Laycock and me looking around the Paris fleamarket - and someone else beating both of us to that red P2 Alfa Romeo

so was he. Looking at his sales table later in the day, I spotted one of the Le Rapide 'Michelin' electric railcars, the model which looks a bit like a road lorry on rails and very often has metal fatigue in the body. This one, however, was as sound as a bell and in absolutely brand new condition with its picture box. The price tag was more than I wanted to pay, but when the Frenchman offered to take the Citroën, pay me the money I had already laid out for it and throw the railcar in for free, I could not resist. In a way it was a shame to see the Citroën go, but I fancied the railcar and it was (as the French dealer put it to me at the time) a very nice "Souvenir de Paris."

As far as the USA and train collecting shows are concerned, there can be nothing to rival the massive Train Collectors' Association's fair in York, Pennsylvania. Anyone who has been there will know how enormous this event is, with hundreds of tables full of old and new trains set out in a number of different halls. As you would expect, American trains dominate and as you walk down the aisles, there are more of these on display than you would ever imagine existed. For anyone not used

Marie and me at the York (Pennsylvania) train show

A gathering of Hornby collectors at the York (Pennsylvania) train show

to all this, spend too long there and you could have recurring nightmares about Lionel trains. They are everywhere.

Amongst all this American hardware, however, are some European trains, especially Märklin but also a sprinkling of Hornby and Bassett-Lowke. I rarely had a sales table there, but it was fun to look around and buy a few things, although prices were never predictable. They tended to be either way over the top or rock bottom, rarely ever in between. You would see a tatty engine out for sale at sky high money and then a real bargain would turn up. I remember buying a Hornby Dublo boxed set with the rare black LNER 0-6-2 tank, complete with the 'Hudson Dobson' import label on the box and in absolutely brand new condition for fifty dollars.

Hornby made a couple of 0 gauge models before the war for the North American market, complete with cowcatcher, and these are now very scarce. Walking round the tables at York, I always expected to turn the very next corner and see one of these sought-after pieces right there for sale, but never ever did. People like John Ridley and Tom Clark have been making pilgrimages to York for years and would probably know exactly where to look for the best items. I believe John found a stack of Hornby Dublo Canadian Pacific tenders at one time, all boxed and unused.

Unlike our events in England, which are usually mixed with both toys and trains, fairs in the United States tend to concentrate on one or the other. Whilst the York show is all trains, fairs in places like Allentown and Chicago are purely for toys. I visited both of these and they were great – plenty of stalls with good items for sale and it was always fun to buy there. At the Chicago fair, I even had a sales table. I had brought only a few pieces over to sell, but I was very much looking forward to seeing how they went. I remember having a 1950s clockwork Donald Duck toy by Schuco in very clean condition, for which I wanted what I felt was a very reasonable two hundred and fifty dollars. As I only had a few pieces on the table, I had not bothered to put price tickets on; I could soon tell anyone how much things were.

For those of us growing up in Britain during the 1950s when our country was still recovering from the economic ravages of war, our impression of America came mostly from the images we would see in the Hollywood films. Here in England, when those people lucky enough to have cars were driving around in Morris Minors and Ford Prefects, just going to the cinema and seeing those enormous chrome covered Buicks and Cadillacs swishing down the highway or pulling into a drive-in movie was like looking in on another world. Consequently, the thought that everyone in America must be loaded with cash is always in the back of your mind. Until that is, the odd thing happens now and again to cause you to question it.

When the doors opened at Chicago, one of the first men to walk in came straight to my table and picked up the Donald Duck. "It's two fifty," I said, fully expecting him to pull out a fist full of dollars and take it without hesitation. I was taken aback when he asked in all sincerity "Is that two hundred and fifty or two dollars fifty?" It got me thinking that 4,000 miles was a long way to come to be asked that question.

The shows in the States were a lot of fun, although I used to treat going over there more as a holiday than anything else – the Donald Duck incident had already warned me that I wasn't cut out to make much money selling there anyway. I mostly enjoyed looking for tin toys for myself, mainly Japanese models of American or British cars. One of the few character toys I bought over there, probably from Allentown, and which I still have, is a Marx clockwork toy of an obviously famous American, Joe Penner. He walks along with both his hat and a big cigar going up and down, holding a duck in one hand and in the other a basket of chicks, with a sign saying "Wanna buy a Duck?" – Where the devil was he when I needed him in Chicago?

I like Americans. Their general laid back, uninhibited 'I'll take things as they come' attitude can sometimes be refreshingly different from ours. You do wonder though whether a few might view 'good old Europe' as simply a branch of the USA. A good many years ago, and well before the Euro currency came in, I remember the London dealer Pete McAskie telling me about the time two very pleasant older American ladies were expressing an interest in one of the toys on his stand in Grays Antiques Market. "How much is this, honey?" was the question. "Two hundred," said Pete. "Is that dollars?" she asked. "No", said Pete. "This is England. Everything here is in pounds." "Hey, now ain't that somethin'?", said the lady. "Last week we were in Paris and everything there was in French francs."

In the United States, Marie and I would usually stay in hotels, and so it was more than a pleasant change on one occasion to stay with Paul Aziz at his house in Connecticut and see his wonderful collection of Bassett-Lowke trains. A Canadian by birth, Paul has been a good friend for many years and a very knowledgeable collector of Bassett-Lowke for even longer. He became interested in British trains as a young man in Canada, and in fact was set on the right path very early in life after being given a Hornby electric 'M' series set as a boy. It was the products of Bassett-Lowke though that really fired his interest in collecting trains and he

Paul Aziz

managed to source a lot of his material in both Canada and the States. Through my selling trains I got to know him very well, especially when he began making regular trips to England.

The nice thing is that we will see a lot more of Paul now that he has left the United States to begin a new life in Europe, with a home here in England and another in Italy. Homes in two countries – now then you see, that proves it – I just knew there was some truth in those Hollywood films.

The only other time we have stayed with friends in the USA was on our first ever trip there in the early 1980s. The late Gates Willard, whom I had known for some time as a very keen collector of Triang Minics and other toys, invited us to stay with him and his lovely wife Evelyn, at their home on Long Island, New York State.

Never having set foot on American soil before, we wanted to visit New York City itself and the very next day after arriving in the US, we took the train from Long Island into Manhattan. After seeing no end of images of New York in films and on television, we were keen to discover how it measured up in the flesh.

We had only just stepped off the train when our first impression of the Big Apple was presented to us exactly as it was so regularly portrayed on the silver screen. Right there in the station was a crowd of people gathered around something on the ground. Homing in closer, we could see that they were all staring intently at a man laid out on the floor. A New York policeman was standing over him and kept shouting "Move back people." Of course it was obvious – the guy had been shot, the cop had finished him off in a shoot-out – just like you would see in the films.

We stood there waiting to see what happened next, when the man on the floor suddenly got to his feet. Apparently he had fainted and someone had called the policeman over to help. I really don't know whether we were more relieved or disappointed.

UNDER THE HAMMER

12

They're not fer laiking wi'

Auction was never a word my grandmother would have used. To her it was always 'the saleroom' and to me she seemed to live there. Her daughter, my mother, did not share her enthusiasm. She saw it only as a place you would visit if you had to, if money was tight and you couldn't afford to buy new. In fact in her eyes there was almost a hint of shame about buying anything from there. My grandmother didn't worry; she loved to buy and would come away from a sale with no end of ornaments, maybe a small table and on one occasion a stuffed bird in a case for a shilling.

As a young boy, she would very often take me to the Ripon saleroom with her, which at that time was located in the town centre, up a flight of wooden steps. I feel certain that it is the vague memory of my visits there with her, the place always busy, lots of people about and plenty going on, that has left me with a fascination for auctions.

Items that had not sold, especially bulky furniture, would often be put outside for anyone to take away for free. This system must have kept the administration simple, although it is hard to imagine today's vendors accepting that arrangement too readily.

If there was something really big to bring back or to take to the saleroom, there was always the horse and cart that belonged to Mr. Simpson, whom I remember calling at my grandmother's house. This was probably an old fashioned way of doing things, even in the 1950s, but my grandmother didn't move quickly with the times.

For one thing, she would never have electricity in the house, although even without this newfangled technology, which everyone else took for granted, she could still receive radio programmes through a service called the Relay. A number of houses in the same road must have been linked in some way to a central broadcasting system. A wooden cased speaker was wired to a wall-mounted metal switch, which you would use to select a station such as the Home Service or the Light Programme. I can remember her listening to the Archers, although never ever sitting down – she would always be doing something else like cooking or cleaning at the same time. She was a lovely lady, who worked hard all her life and her house still had gas lighting when she died in 1965.

Marie and I have long shared an interest in auctions, and many has been the time that we have looked in at a viewing somewhere, only to walk straight out again after five minutes if nothing catches the eye, but you never know, it is always fun to look. We were in Whitby some years ago, and were walking past a building which we hadn't realised at first was a saleroom, not to mention an auction actually in progress, until we caught the sound of the auctioneer's voice over a crowd of people standing in the doorway. It was clear that the place was absolutely packed, which made us all the more curious and we managed to squeeze through into the hall so we could see exactly what was going on.

The auctioneer was really zipping away – "fifty fifty, sixty sixty, seventy seventy, eighty eighty, ninety ninety" followed by the loud bang of the hammer coming down and then "Sold – ninety pence." No end of lots would go through in a similar vein, with just the occasional one topping the pound mark. As I remarked to Marie, we had found our level at last. It is funny how you can often go to a sale where every lot is selling for hundreds of pounds and there might only be a dozen people in the room. Then you come across an auction like the Whitby one, simply heaving with people and a lot of the stuff is being knocked down for a pound or less. Sometimes it can be almost a reverse ratio of people to prices. You would imagine the sheer number of folks in the room would force the prices up, but it doesn't seem to work like that.

Selling cheaply here were mainly trays of ornaments, glasses and a few lots the auctioneer would describe as 'A box of miscellaneous items'. Not exactly a description to put the auction staff's cataloguing skills to the test. On the other hand, unless there was only one item actually in the box, there could be no danger of the buyer complaining afterwards that the lot was not as described. All the activity going on had certainly drawn the two of us into the saleroom and we took a fancy to a couple of lots which were coming up later, including a ship's wheel which now stands in our bathroom. He failed to stop at ninety pence for that unfortunately, but it seemed a decent buy all the same.

Sometime around 1985, my mother told me about a sale she knew would be coming up shortly in Ripon. An old gentleman living in the same large terraced house since before the war had died and the contents were due to be auctioned. He was one of those people who had never thrown much away (obviously a true Yorkshireman). Unfortunately, his hoarding had extended to dozens of unopened bottles of milk, even more outdated cans of food, mountains of newspapers and other equally useless items which, once the auctioneers got to work, went straight into a large skip outside the house. Aside from all the rubbish though were some nice pieces of antique furniture and a whole stack of pre-war toys.

The toys included a large amount of early Hornby 0 gauge trains, Hornby Dublo and Dinky Toys. The highlight for me, however, was a stack of about twenty pre-war novelty biscuit tins, many still with their original boxes, including motor cars, trains and other rarities. These were not things the Ripon saleroom regulars would normally expect to see, and it tickled me during the viewing to observe two old gentlemen weighing up what was on offer. "There's some toys 'ere", said one to his friend, who countered "Aye, but they're not fer laiking wi'."

The toys there were great, but as usual I was not the only person in the room interested. Nowadays, with the power of the internet, everyone seems to get to know about every toy that turns up at every sale anywhere in the country and although that was not the case back then, it still felt like it. With any one of these out of the way auctions, where a few nice toys or trains would be sprinkled among all the furniture, ornaments and pots and pans, it was very often the same scenario. All the way driving to the sale, you would be thinking – with a bit of luck there won't be much competition, I can't imagine too many people knowing about this – I could have a field day.

Then, when you finally arrived, you would walk through the door and be immediately confronted by every single person within a hundred-mile radius who could possibly be interested, all there at the viewing and each one saying to the other "What are you doing here?" Even though it was the middle of winter and snow was on the ground, there was still plenty of that going on at this sale. Nevertheless, I managed to come away with some nice things, including quite a few of the biscuit tins and, maybe as a sweetener for Marie, a small clock and a jardiniere and stand.

As it happens, prices at this auction were not ridiculously high, which was a nice change because so often with these type of auctions, where toys come up only infrequently, more seasoned auction-goers will be outbid by a local person determined to buy. Some collectors seeing items even only loosely of interest coming up in a sale near to home will often feel a compulsion to own them. The price these things might be worth when considered in the cold light of day simply doesn't come into it – they have to be bought. I have been witness to many situations where someone has paid far more for a toy or train in a their local saleroom than they would ever have done elsewhere. Had the same item turned up in a specialist toy auction, or been out for sale at a fair somewhere, he or she would not have dreamt of buying it in the first place, never mind pay all the money they had done in the local auction.

The fact of the matter is that when it comes to buying, we can all be influenced by the particular situation. No matter how much of a sensible, reasoned thinker any of us might like to think we are and how subjective we try to be, any item can appear more or less attractive to us, depending on where it might be for sale, or indeed, who is selling.

The first auction I was involved in actually organising was a joint effort with Ron Budd. The sale date was 20th October 1980 and the venue, the Cavendish Hotel in Eastbourne. Ron is one of those people who, as everyone acquainted with him must agree, never ever seems to age. He has looked exactly the same to me during all the

Ron and Angela Budd (right) with Mike and Sheila Brown at
The London Toy and Model Museum Fair

time I have known him. A long time collector, and together with his wife Angela, he was a regular at fairs up and down the country for many years. The two of them take things more leisurely now, which they are entitled to do, but a lot of train events don't seem quite the same without them both.

The rostrum duty in Eastbourne was divided up between the Reverend Tom Tyler and myself. I suppose that, for a vicar, the prospect of being up front conducting a sale might not seem too dissimilar from delivering a sermon, even though Tom would be more used to a congregation holding hymn sheets rather than bidding numbers. For me, however, it was my very first time with the gavel and likely the only occasion I will ever get to share the job with a man of the cloth. I cannot remember too much about the day itself, although I must have been a bit nervous. I still have a catalogue from the sale, showing a Hornby 0 gauge streamlined train set in maroon and cream with original box which made £120 and also in 0 gauge a boxed Hornby clockwork 'Yorkshire' locomotive and tender, which sold for £280.

Perhaps it was because Ron Budd and I lived so far apart that we did not manage to arrange more auctions together, but after the Eastbourne adventure, another friend of mine David Smith from Kettering approached me regarding auctions. He told me about Lilford Hall, a country house near Thrapston in Northamptonshire. The titled owner was living abroad, but David was friendly with the owner's agent, who was looking after the house and grounds in his absence. He, in turn, introduced us to two men who were using Lilford Hall as a Business and Conference Centre and they were keen to hold other events there. It was a great venue, a large impressive house in spacious grounds. Everything seemed exactly right, so we arranged a date with them for our first auction, Sunday 1st November 1981.

As David and I were not known for running auctions, the lots did not exactly come flooding in. Nevertheless, through advertising, obtaining items from collectors we knew and adding in some things of our own, we managed to put together a very respectable sale of 214 decent lots. The catalogue shows a number of boxed Hornby Dublo locomotives together with a Southern Tank set, a Trix 'Princess' boxed set, a boxed Hornby 0 gauge electric 'Eton' locomotive, a rare Bassett-Lowke class 5 locomotive, Meccano cars, boxed Dinky Toys and an unusual Märklin station. Whilst for that hard to satisfy person looking for something a little different, there was a French First World War tinplate Army Knackers Van (it was for transporting dead horses), of which I have yet to see another.

The response from buyers to the sale was encouraging and we had a good crowd there including Anthony Bianco, David Burt, Irving Brim, Bob Scott, Stuart Bean and many others. In fact, Stuart mentioned this auction in conversation with me

Conducting the auction at Lilford Hall

only recently and said "Do you remember Simon Goodyear arrived late?". I hadn't remembered, but there is something nicely reassuring about knowing that reputations such as this have been honestly earned and fairly attributed, and can be traced back a fair way. I don't have a list of prices realised from the sale, although going from memory an illuminated Hornby Dublo display sign made £110, the Märklin station £420, the Bassett-Lowke engine £700 and the Knackers van about £120. Everyone seemed to enjoy the day and some said they hoped that we would do another.

Immediately the auction had finished, we found the two men in charge of the conference side of things, standing in the entrance hall waiting to see us. It had already been agreed that we would be settling with them for the hire of the rooms

Simon helping at Lilford Hall

sometime after the day, but now they were asking if we could pay in cash there and then. With the takings from the sale, we had enough to do it, so we settled up, thanked them for having us and took our leave. Within less than a week it became clear why they had insisted on cash. The two of them had been arrested for serious fraud and the whole of Lilford Hall had been boarded up and sealed off by the police. After having had no end of alterations and building work done in the house, the conference business had not taken off and a great deal of money apparently was owed.

As we reflected afterwards, if the auction had been arranged for just one week later, it could not possibly have taken place at all. About two or three years later, when things had calmed down, my son Simon and I met up with the owner's agent again and arranged a couple of Vintage Toy Collectors Fairs at Lilford Hall. The auction, however, turned out to be a one-off.

David and I had enjoyed organising it and of course that is the important thing. Making a little money as well would not have gone too far amiss, but that was not so easy to do. I don't believe we lost anything on the exercise, but after advertising costs, the money for room hire and everything else, we came out about even. Our plan all along had been to arrange more auctions, but after weighing up the amount of work we had put in and the struggle we had to attract enough quality items, it seemed as though we would be facing an uphill battle to get things really singing and dancing.

As anyone who has ever started an auction from scratch will verify, it does take time for people to have enough confidence in what you are doing before the items start to roll in. I dare say we could have continued and sold items of mine, but what would have been the point, when I could sell them just as easily myself without the trouble and expense of arranging an auction? As it was, we were too impatient to wait for things to build up. David had other things to do and I was happy buying and selling trains and running the toy fairs. We called it a day and put the whole thing down to being a fun experience. More than ten years would pass before I started to think about delving into the world of auctions again.

David Smith and me at the Lilford Hall Auction

UNDER THE HAMMER

13

Hornby Dublo anyone?

Early in 1992, I was offered the opportunity of acquiring a unique collection. This was the majority of the original records, photographs, share certificates, postcards, blueprints of models, films and no end of other material from the archives of the Bassett-Lowke Company. Inherited by the new owner of Bassett-Lowke, the collection had survived despite a number of company moves and changes in ownership. I bought the collection and although I wanted to keep many of the items myself, I had neither the desire nor the space to hold onto everything. There was

W.J. Bassett-Lowke's own share certificate

simply too much – literally thousands of photographs and all manner of documents. It was a fascinating collection, and as these items were truly unique, after selecting the items I wanted, it occurred to me that an auction would be the ideal way to sell the remainder. Before going down that particular avenue, however, I knew I would definitely need help from at least one of my sons.

Simon had been working with Marie and myself running the fairs for some years. He was enjoying organising the fairs, and had more appetite for developing that side of things than getting involved with an auction as well. Ellis, on the other hand was much keener on the idea and thought that an auction of toys and trains could work, maybe even on a regular basis. He was not personally involved with the fairs at that time. He had been busy buying and selling Hornby Dublo trains.

As far as I was concerned, although I had enjoyed dealing in trains for years, the gloss had begun to fade. As with so many things in life, most of us tend to compare the current state of play with earlier times. If I had just been starting out on my dealing career, no doubt I would have happily adapted to the situation as it was at the time. But as I had enjoyed such a long period when the buying and selling seemed far easier and less competitive than it was becoming, my enthusiasm for dealing was receding. The more I thought about starting an auction, the more attractive it seemed.

In the early 1990s, other than Vectis who were very strong in diecast and the sales at Lacy Scott's in Bury St. Edmunds, if you wanted to buy toys and trains at auction you had no choice other than to look towards the sales in London. Travelling into the capital, especially in the week, has always had its drawbacks and at that time these sales did not usually attract a multitude of buyers. Apart from the dealers and a number of dedicated collectors based in and around London, it seemed to us that there were many people out there who for one reason or another were not being drawn to these auctions. We felt sure that if we had a regular auction in a place that was easy to reach, with sales held on a weekend so that more people could attend, there would be every chance of success.

I already had a venue in mind. We had been using Rugby's Benn Hall for fairs since 1980 and for a long time it had struck me as perfect for an auction. In the very centre of the country, next to the M1 and M6 motorways, plenty of car parking, close to a main line railway station, a large stage area and with a side room for serving refreshments – the place seemed tailor made.

Ellis and I discussed all conceivable angles and issues many times in order to thrash out a format we thought was workable. We were certain that a Saturday auction would be best and viewing on the morning of the sale should be enough. To be frank, I have always considered long viewing times unnecessary. In my experience, a shorter time concentrates the mind much more and avoids putting the lots at extra risk from too much handling. As the Benn Hall was a large venue for an auction, we felt that having sales tables in the room would add something to the day, and at the same time offset the cost of hiring the hall.

Whilst the Bassett-Lowke archive material gave us the nucleus of a sale, we needed more quality items, if we were to make a good impression with this first auction. Again, just like Lilford Hall ten years earlier, it was not exactly a doddle amassing the required number of lots. In the end, with a combination of items from people we knew and some things of mine, we had 351 lots, 186 of which were the Bassett-Lowke records. The catalogue was A5 size with a card cover, photocopied colour pictures in the centre and a photograph depicting a selection of the Bassett-Lowke archive material attached to the front. To keep costs down to a minimum, we came back from the copy shop with the loose pages, covers and front photographs and had a production line operation at home to put everything together. About 350 catalogues were ready for the first sale.

Saturday 10th October 1992 was the date of the inaugural Barry Potter Auction at the Benn Hall. Tables, microphone and other ancillary items were put in place during the Friday afternoon and we came along around 6am on auction day to set up the lots themselves.

The day itself came and went without any real problems. Prices for the Bassett-Lowke archive items varied like chalk and cheese, from £900 for the collection of films to £2 each for batches of photographs of model buildings made by the firm. It was a collection we had decided was to be sold without reserve, and when that is the case and values and level of interest are difficult to gauge, it is interesting to see just where prices finish up. Some of these lots, like the photographs, were going for bargain prices and then a collection of postcards showing model and miniature railways would be contested right up to more than £800. On the more predictable side, a very nice collection of Hornby tanker wagons sold well and a Bassett-Lowke live steam 'Flying Scotsman' in gauge 1 made £1,900. We were in the auction business.

Happy enough with the way this first sale had gone, beginning in January 1993 we arranged four more dates for that year. The catalogue format remained much the same, with groups of items pictured on a shelf system, photocopied colour pages inside and a colour photograph on the cover. Within three years or so we graduated from photocopied pages to having the catalogues printed and more colour pictures inside. No longer having to staple everything together, it was great just to go down

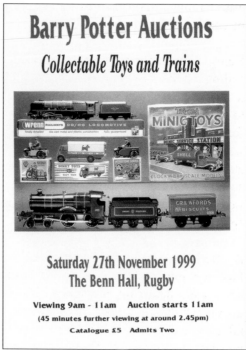

The first Rugby catalogue from 1992   The final A5 sized catalogue

to the printers and collect the whole lot finished and ready to go. The catalogues were starting to look much better and for the last two or three years of having the A5 size we thought they looked quite snazzy.

Having decided finally to cease dealing in trains and with Ellis fully committed and the two of us working together, unlike the situation more than ten years earlier at Lilford, we were prepared to put in the time and effort to make the venture a success. As more and more people were beginning to like what we were doing, good collections were slowly starting to come in. At first, there was probably only just enough to keep us comfortably full from sale to sale, but before too long the trickle became more of a flow.

Something which dawned on me during this period was the gradual realisation that all those little bits of knowledge, experience, feel, call it what you like, that I must have acquired without thinking about it through years of collecting and dealing in trains were now being put to another use. Suddenly, all that time I had spent having fun buying and selling trains was not just discarded and forgotten; it was proving useful right now in dealing with vendors and with cataloguing the sales. Perhaps after having a number of different jobs in earlier life, it was nice to have some sort of continuity to what I was doing.

Being a dealer for so long, it was a little strange at first talking to someone about selling a collection on his or her behalf, when at one time I would have been trying to buy it. Having had so many years buying and selling, however, it was refreshing to be looking at things from another perspective. As an auctioneer, it is far easier for sellers to accept you as someone to do business with. This is particularly true with sellers you meet for the first time, who naturally feel that you are on their side anyway. Of course, all the best dealers inspire confidence and have clients who will accept their advice above all else, which is a great compliment to them. I am not saying that there is anything better or worse about being an auctioneer and acting simply as an agent, it is sometimes just a lot easier.

As my buying and selling trains had finished soon after starting the Rugby auctions, I had nothing much left to sell apart from anything in my own collection. Having been known as a dealer for ever and a day, I suppose it was only to be expected that some people would still think of me in that role for a while. Nevertheless, it was amusing after we had been running the auctions for about five years when someone asked me whether everything in a forthcoming sale was mine. I should have been flattered that he would imagine me having such a fabulous stock of trains – for to be able to fill five sales a year for five years and still be going strong, I would certainly have needed one.

It is a funny thing about the ownership of items being sold at auction. If the collection coming up for sale is a special one, headlined by the owner's name, then of course the whole thing is out in the open for everyone to see and indeed pieces in a good quality sale of this kind can do very well. Buyers will often relate strongly to a named collection, with items making perhaps a little more than they might in a more usual auction. Outside of the named or titled collection sales, however, confidentiality is the keyword. If a vendor chooses to tell someone a collection is being sold on their behalf, that is their choice, but the auctioneer of course cannot.

With auctions, we very quickly learned that, if asked whether a particular item or collection belonged to whoever, the safest answer was "No", whatever the reality might be. Any response such as "I could not possibly say" can, even without intention, be almost a confirmation. The confidential nature surrounding sellers does actually help the sale, for were it ever a legal requirement to include sellers' names in the catalogue, there is no doubt that prices would suffer. Other than the special collection sales headed up with the vendor's name as mentioned earlier, most people would find it difficult to be entirely subjective about bidding for something if the owner was someone known to them, however vaguely. In common with so many things in life, most of us respond very well to a little bit of mystery.

For the January 1994 auction, we had two collections of note. The first one was of a make with which we were very familiar – Hornby Dublo. The vendor, whom I had known for years, had collected everything in absolutely superb boxed condition, but a little more unusual was the fact that almost every piece was duplicated. With shades of Noah and the Ark, there were two examples of everything including all the rare locomotives in both 2- and 3-rail, together with the entire range of super detail rolling stock.

Our quandary was whether to present the entire collection in a single sale, or to split it over two. Selling the collection in two sections would have been the easy option; that way there was no danger of saturating the market. Who wants the easy way though? Our gut feeling was that the one-sale approach would be better, on the basis that having two of each item would encourage more bidders to enter the fray, sensing they had more chance of success. We felt that having everything in the one sale would have more impact and was likely to bring more buyers out of the woodwork. This, then, was the way we chose to go.

The second collection in the sale was of Wrenn Railways; in fact no less than sixty-four locomotives and almost all mint and boxed. We were familiar with Wrenn in general, and models such as 'Cardiff Castle' and 'City of London' we had seen many times before. Frankly though, we had not appreciated that the range was so big and many of the other names, such as 'Lord Dowding', 'Biggin Hill', 'Dominion of Canada' and 'Princess Alice' we were simply unaware of. The collection had been consigned to us through a friend acting as agent for the vendor, and we were told that if this first consignment went well, there was as much again to follow.

The agent informed us that his client was insistent on fixed reserves with little discretion and, although he kept assuring us that everything would be fine, we remained far from convinced. As it added up to a fair amount of money, assuming we could sell it, this was not a collection we wanted to turn away. Nevertheless, we were slightly nervous and feared that there could be much left unsold. We catalogued the two collections, deciding to sell the Hornby Dublo first, followed by the Wrenn.

As soon as the catalogues were out, the interest that was being expressed in the Wrenn was incredible. Bids by fax and post were arriving every day. People were telephoning asking all kinds of questions and all for a collection we thought could well have spelled trouble. As we very soon discovered, there was a good reason for all the attention. The collection could not have been sold at a better time, for the Wrenn company had closed its doors for business only a year or so earlier and the interest in these trains, which

were no longer being produced, had soared. It seemed as though everyone in the world had suddenly switched on to collecting Wrenn at the same time.

After a while, all the concerns we once had about the Wrenn were directed elsewhere. Almost every bid coming in and almost every telephone enquiry was to do with Wrenn. What about Hornby Dublo? Hardly anyone was asking about it. Here we were, with this fabulous collection coming up for sale and, with all the attention centred on Wrenn, it seemed as if everything else had been forgotten.

Worse still, because the Hornby Dublo would be sold first, we had this nightmare scenario in our minds of everyone sitting in the auction room, with arms firmly by their sides all the way through the Hornby Dublo. Every single person waiting for the Wrenn and all watching impassively as the Dublo was being knocked down for next to nothing. If only we had put the Wrenn on first we thought. We were uneasy about the whole business.

When the day finally came, we felt much more than just relief to see the Hornby Dublo selling well. Sure, we had nothing like the number of pre-sale bids that had been lodged for the Wrenn, but there were plenty of buyers in the room and the bidding was strong. For example, the two 'City of Liverpool' locomotives went for £580 and £480, 'Ludlow Castle' £420 and £520, the 2-6-4 tanks '80059' £520 and £500, the E3002 locomotives £520 and £480 and the Rail Cleaning Wagons £680 and £520. These were strong prices and ones I would say most sellers would be more than happy to achieve today.

It was just so pleasing to see people out there still wanting good old Hornby Dublo. Whether we were right to put the whole collection in the one sale we will never know – it was an interesting dilemma. In reality it probably made little difference, although looking at the prices, I believe it was the right decision.

After all the pre-sale interest, it came as no surprise to see the Wrenn selling strongly. The 'Lord Dowding' for which the £180-240 estimate had at one time really concerned us, made £400, the 'Seaton' also £400, 'King George VI' £520 and 'Queen Elizabeth' £440. The second half of the collection eventually arrived and formed part of the next auction. With it the interest increased even further. This was the start of many years of selling Wrenn at Rugby and it is fair to say that our auction became well known as the place to buy and sell it. Goodness knows, in locomotives alone, how much Wrenn has passed through the Benn Hall doors since that day, but with sixty or seventy engines in most sales since then, it will run into thousands.

The auction was very much a family business, with us working from home. Marie was a big help with the administrative side, before, during and after the sale day, whilst Ellis and myself would deal with clients, do the cataloguing and any other jobs needed. We had a large, secure double garage where we stored the lots and carried out the cataloguing work.

The strange thing with auctions is how things can quickly fluctuate from a position of you wondering (even praying maybe) when the next collections are going to be arriving, to you wondering when they are going to stop. Once collections began to come in steadily, we established a pattern of working that led up to each sale. It was important to us from the outset to maximise the value of each auction. We always felt that if we were to go through all the cataloguing operation and everything else which needed to be done before and after the day, every auction had to be as worthwhile as we could make it. It never made sense to us to spread items over two sales if we could fit the same amount into one.

During the last years of our running the business, the hammer prices for each of our five auctions a year were averaging around £150,000. Trains were the mainstay and while 0 gauge items were generally relied on for high values, Wrenn and, to a lesser degree Hornby Dublo, were usually the easiest to catalogue.

Ellis and I would work together, reckoning generally that from examining items to finalising the descriptions and making up the trays or boxes ready for sale, we could complete around sixty lots per day. Some items were easier to process than others, mixed low value items usually being the worst. Whenever it looked as though sixty lots was going to be difficult to achieve on a particular day, we would try to find something easier, like a batch of Wrenn engines, to move things along a bit quicker. It was always a question of dates and deadlines to meet, working back from the day of the auction itself. Lot descriptions would be keyed directly into a computer and, once cataloguing was complete, we would trawl through the lots and select items for photography.

This was before digital photography was popular and we used a Canon 35mm SLR camera, with the catalogue illustrations taken directly from colour prints. It was always a mixture of thrill and trepidation when the catalogues came back from the printers. After spending the best part of the previous month, some days working until midnight to get the cataloguing finished, we wanted the printed end product to be as good as we could make it.

I suppose the perception that there is money to be made from selling auction catalogues is an easy one to believe. Easy that is, unless you happen to be someone involved in running an auction. We didn't have all that many sales under our belt at Rugby when I remember someone telling me precisely how much he reckoned Roger Mazillius at Vectis was making on the sales of his catalogues at every auction. Aware of our own experience with the costs involving catalogues, I simply could not believe it. Soon afterwards I mentioned this to Roger. He laughed and told me that, ironically, the amount in question was almost exactly how much he was actually losing on them.

Losing, of course, is not strictly the correct business term here. The cost of catalogue production is just another necessary expense for auction houses, like staffing costs, advertising or whatever else. Being able to sell some of the catalogues to prospective bidders merely defrays some of those costs. For any auction house, the sales income from catalogues very seldom if ever covers the cost of producing them.

Apart from the vendors who receive theirs free, the reduced catalogue prices for everyone on the subscription list and the ever rising cost of postage, there are those people who have a distinct aversion to paying for catalogues. It would take Ellis and I the best part of maybe four weeks to catalogue and photograph items for a sale. When the catalogues were back from the printers, we would send the ones out which needed to be posted and then finally, we would take some to sell at the very next fair we were going to. After we had been working flat out for the last month to get the catalogue ready and then having paid the printer's bill for goodness knows how much, the same routine would always follow.

At the fair, we would wait in eager anticipation, certain that anyone even remotely interested would seize upon this literary gem we had been slaving on for weeks, whip out their wallet and snap up the catalogue in sheer delight. Then, by the end of the day, after we had seen perhaps a dozen people or more pick it up and read through from cover to cover, before carefully placing it down again and walking off, we would remember how things actually were in the real world.

Do not misunderstand me here. The great majority of serious auction buyers are usually more than happy to buy catalogues or to take out subscriptions, and of course most auction houses will try to price their catalogues as low as they possibly can, in order to place them into the hands of potential buyers. After saying that, however, there are more than a few people who at auction would think nothing of bidding £800, £900, £1,000, or whatever it takes. Then, on another day the very same person would say "How much is that catalogue? £5! Come on! Give me a break. I'm not made of money." The amazing thing is that every person like this thinks that they are the only one. The reason I know they are not alone is because I used to be just as bad myself.

The best thing now of course for us natural cheapskates is the listing of auction catalogues on the internet, where everything can be seen for free. Now and again you will see someone walk into an auction room with a four-inch thick computer print out of the entire catalogue. The fact that the printing ink used to produce this has probably cost three times as much as the catalogue would have done in the first place is beside the point – the price of the catalogue has been saved.

Trains were our speciality, but now and again it was great to have a collection of other toys to sell, especially diecast models in top condition. Not only were they easier to catalogue, but compared to the drab appearance of so many of the trains, they looked so colourful and attractive in the catalogue pictures. After struggling with a collection of say mixed 00 gauge trains, which needed a fair amount of sorting into lots before the cataloguing could even start, it was a piece of cake to process a collection of mint boxed Dinky or Corgi Toys which we could rattle off in no time. Tin toys were also nice to have; boats, cars or whatever. All of these things were such a change from the trains we had coming in all the while.

Another factor was the space that trains took up, particularly 0 gauge and larger ones. They compared badly with things like Dinky Toys, which you could often fit into a couple of shoe boxes. To transport the auction lots to Rugby, we invariably needed to hire a large Luton van. Once it was packed, you would struggle to fit another toy or train in. I remember Roger Mazillius from Vectis Auctions, after he had driven what he described to me as "a massive sale of diecast models" down to Guildford, telling me that the lots stacked up so high they were within six inches of the roof of his tiny Mazda van. I don't reckon these diecast guys really know what hard work is all about.

UNDER THE HAMMER

14

Pass me that telephone

Looking back through the catalogues brings to mind some of the vendors whom we dealt with at the time. A man from Cumbria had called in to see us with his Hornby Dublo trains from childhood – a 'Duchess of Montrose' boxed set, wagons etc. It was all standard stuff, nothing to write home about, and he was not surprised when we told him that it might make £150 or thereabouts. Then he mentioned something else he wasn't sure was going to be worth putting in, and pulled out a 1914 Meccano Steam Engine. Rare enough on its own perhaps, but this one was complete with the original strawboard box. After him asking us if it might make £25, I told him to leave it to us and he could well be surprised.

When it finally came up in the sale, the interest was unreal. Few people had ever seen an original box before and the hammer came down at a staggering £1,920. About four weeks later, the vendor called me on the phone and said that he was a bit concerned, because we had obviously sent him the wrong cheque for the steam engine. After I told him that there was definitely no mistake, he must have wondered just what sort of a crazy world we were living in.

As every dealer in Hornby 0 gauge trains would testify, anyone who is in possession of a 'Princess Elizabeth' locomotive, especially one which they have had from childhood, invariably feels that they are holding the next best thing to the crown jewels. The pinnacle of the Hornby range and in the wooden presentation case, it does of course look superb. Being so comparatively expensive when new (more than £5 in 1938) and with the presentation box as protection has meant that most were well looked after. Indeed, it is precisely because they were cherished that so many have survived. Consequently, they are not quite as rare, and therefore as valuable, as some owners might imagine or even some television programmes would like us to believe.

It was a nice, but frankly in no way brilliant example that a man had brought in for Ellis and I to look at. After receiving the model for Christmas in 1938, he had finally decided that now was the time to sell. We told him that it would probably make around £1,200 and might do a little better, if we were lucky. Not unexpectedly, he was hoping for more, something nearer the £2,000 a friend had told him these were definitely worth. We assured the owner that we would do the best we could, although we would not feel too happy about taking the model with a reserve of more than £1,100, which in the end he agreed to.

Just before we gave him the receipt, and almost as an afterthought, he mentioned some Hornby accessories he had brought along in the car boot. We walked outside together and he lifted the boot lid to reveal seven green boxes of electrically lit Hornby accessories – a Signal Gantry, Goods Depot, Station, two Lamp Standards, a small Level Crossing and a Water Tank. These represented seven of the most desirable Hornby items you could ask for, and all in top boxed condition. As he clearly did not regard them as having too much worth, we were convinced that his disappointment over our valuation of the 'Princess' would very soon be forgotten.

When it came to the auction, the 'Princess Elizabeth' made £1,400, the Station £250, two Lamp Standards £720, Level Crossing £200, Goods Depot £950, Water Tank £2,250 and the Signal Gantry £3,200. After the sale and once he had received his cheque, he phoned me to thank us, and said that he was absolutely amazed and delighted with the prices of the accessories. He said it was staggering; he simply could not believe how much they had made. Then, just before he hung up, his parting words to us were "But I did think the Princess might have done a bit better."

It is always pleasing to achieve a good result at auction for a vendor whom you have dealt with personally, or have known beforehand. The Water Tank in the car boot reminded me of one that I had sold in my train dealing days to a very good friend, who at the time was building a layout of Hornby trains. I cannot recall whether it was £100 or £125 he paid, but it was something like that anyway. Years later, when we were running the auction and he was moving from Hornby 0 gauge to gauge 1, we sold quite a number of items for him, although he was always reluctant to let go of the Water Tank. I told him that he should let us have it, because it could make a thousand pounds. It was an item you rarely saw and never with the original box. On that basis, he relented, we put it through and it sold for £2,700. A friend of mine commented recently that when you look at the prices today, we should have kept all those trains we had years ago. He probably had a point, but where exactly would be the fun in that?

The late Jim Whittaker, whom I had first met outside a Bradford train shop many years earlier and got to know much better since, had asked us to sell his collection.

THE CHEEK OF IT – ERECTING A BUS STOP RIGHT OUTSIDE OUR HOUSE

By Jim Whittaker

Jim was an immensely talented model maker and winner of a number of awards for his work, including two of the prestigious Model Engineer gold medals – one for each of his two incredibly detailed brass models of Great Western wagons.

Jim always had a soft spot for Marie. They got on very well and indeed were pen friends for a long time, when he would often send her one of his hand drawn cartoons, featuring trains or collecting characters. Being a fan of the Great Western Railway he often adopted as his pen name that of the famous engineer, Daniel Gooch. Jim, being a very generous man and using his engineering skills, wanted to make something special for Marie and decided on a pair of earrings. They were superbly constructed and must be the ultimate accessory for the wife of a train man, for I just cannot imagine that there can be another lady anywhere in the world with a pair of earrings modelled as railway screw link couplings.

Jim's engineering skills were second to none, but it was his commercially made tinplate models he wanted us to sell. They were all wanted and they sold well enough, and it was through Jim's later recommendation that we dealt with three or four good collections belonging to people he knew.

On one occasion we travelled to the Manchester area to see the trains which had belonged to one of his friends who had recently passed away. The old gentleman had lived in a large Victorian house, once apparently very much admired by the Coronation Street actress Julie Goodyear. The family told us that she had called round several times imploring the old man to sell the house to her, and every single time he would shoo her away with a very firm "No!" Things rarely work out perfectly of course. After he died and the family finally wanted to sell, there was no sign of Julie Goodyear as a buyer. She must have found somewhere else, for the house was to remain on the market for some time.

On our visit there, Marie had taken a liking to an ornamental wheelbarrow standing out in the garden and the son promised that he would speak to the rest of the family and ask if they would consider selling it to us. In the meantime, in the same way that he used to clamber underneath real railway wagons inspecting every possible detail before making his scale models, Jim had been over to the house and had measured every inch of that wheelbarrow, before constructing a miniature model in wood and metal to present to Marie. Jim's kind thought was just as well, for by the

Jim Whittaker (centre) and Peter Phillips examine a Hornby engine at
The Great Central Railway Fair in 1990

time the family had finally decided that they would part with the wheelbarrow after all, it had been pinched. Nothing to do with us, I hasten to add.

After discussing the train collection with the son, it was agreed that we would take everything away. We were packed up and preparing to leave when he remembered a metal chest in a top room we had yet to look in. I prised open the lid to find it crammed full of rare Bassett-Lowke train accessories, obviously all salted away by the old man years earlier. Included there were three of the 1930s Bassett-Lowke personality figures, each mint in its own little box. One was of George Bernard Shaw, but the one to really grab my attention was none other than that of Mr. Bassett-Lowke himself. I had come across examples of these figures before, although rarely with original boxes and never had I seen a figure of the famous model maker.

I had not managed to buy very much for my own collection for some time, but this was one item I really would have liked. As these items were destined for the auction, however, it was impossible. There is nothing wrong in buying something from a sale you are involved in, but as this figure would have been something I might have fancied showing off afterwards, rightly or wrongly I did not feel too comfortable about it. I was imagining putting it out on display somewhere and someone saying "I bet the hammer came down quick that time." In a situation like that, it is difficult to win.

In the end, Mr. Bassett-Lowke sold for £360 to a friend of mine, who is a keen collector of these figures. Afterwards, I thought "Well, at least it was nice to see it and to have it in the sale." I assumed that I wouldn't see another example mint in the box, and resigned myself to that.

It can only have been a year or so later when a man walked into our toy fair in Kettering. He had a few small train items he wanted to sell, including nothing less than a Mr. Bassett-Lowke figure in absolutely brand new condition and complete with the box – every bit as perfect as the first one. I could not believe it. He asked me whether anyone might be interested. I just looked him in the eye and said "I'm your man."

There is no doubt whatsoever in my mind that, for anyone involved in this business of auctions, even more important than being whiter than white is to be perceived as being so. Whilst you can try to do everything as correctly as possible, anything newly introduced can still attract a little suspicion. At Rugby, for a long time the only bidding from people not actually present in the room were commission bids left on the book. As a result, I remember very well an incident on the very day we

W. J. B....... -L....

A well-known figure in the
model world.

"Always on the Move."

Mr. Bassett-Lowke himself

introduced live bidding by telephone. A good friend of mine, whom I know will not mind my reporting this because we have joked about it since, was bidding away when suddenly a member of staff handling the telephone bids raised his arm. A little taken aback by this, my friend momentarily stopped bidding. After I had taken two or three bids from the person holding the telephone and from someone else in the room, my friend re-entered the bidding and managed to secure the lot.

At the end of the sale, he asked me in all seriousness if there really had been anyone on the other end of the telephone. Which, when you think about it, is quite a question. I told him that no, we really hadn't arranged to have someone standing there with a dummy telephone in order for us to take fictitious bids whenever we fancied. How do you prove it, though? I suppose you could always pass the handset round in turn to everyone in the room. In that way they could each have a word and then be happy that they were bidding against a real person. Even then – who is to say that the person on the end of the line really is genuine and not someone just pretending to be a customer, or even a Russian secret agent trying to infiltrate the world of Hornby Dublo?

Unfortunately, there are a few people who do not relish coming up against a bidder on the telephone. You can have a person who will start to bid and take on anyone else in the room, arm waving vigorously in the air, all the way to the price needed, and so far there is no problem at all. Then, as soon as the telephone bidder comes in, the same arm is down like a flash of lightning and the contest stops there and then. There is no doubt that some people have the distinct impression that the person on the end of the telephone has to be a really big spender. Almost certainly an American, sat there in Beverley Hills, feet up with a massive cigar, prepared to go to whatever money it takes.

Quite recently at a lunch for about a dozen fellow collectors, we got to talking about telephone bidding at auctions. I mentioned about the image of the big spender and added that the person on the end of the phone was more likely to be just a regular guy from Derby. At that, a friend of mine almost choked on his bread roll and quipped "Hey watch it – I'm from Derby."

Commission bids left on the book are usually straightforward, and contrary to what some people might think, most auctioneers will not start at the top of the bid. Like most things in life I dare say there will be exceptions to the rule, but the majority of auction houses are not into making a quick killing – they want your business long term. They know full well that anyone who leaves absentee bids and finds that their maximum price has been paid every time will not be bidding that way for much longer. Auction houses are no different from any other business, in that they want to see their customers coming back time and time again.

Occasionally, however, a seemingly unassailable one-off bid on the book can be put to the test in the room. One particular train lot at Rugby sticks in my mind. It was an item similar to many we had seen in previous sales and around £150 would have been the most you would normally have expected to pay. Our estimate in fact, was not unduly low at £80-£120. Before auction day a commission bid was lodged at a hefty £500. When the lot came up in the sale, after starting off at the estimate, someone in the room took it on bid by bid against the commission all the way up to £480.

I took the last bid available on the book at £500, at which point the man in the room hesitated, thought about it for at least two or three seconds, then shook his head. I was thinking to myself, "Go on. Have another bid. Don't land me with this and have the commission bidder feel he has been run up." Disappointingly, the man in the room was obviously not a mind reader, as he made no further movement and the hammer fell at £500. After the sale, I remember feeling it necessary to call the commission buyer on the telephone and explain the situation. That is just how daft it can get.

When it comes to bidding increments, if you thought that one £10 or £20 increment should not matter too much either way, you would be very wrong, especially when dealers are involved. After successfully bidding for something, a dealer might say afterwards "Oh yeah, dead right that was. I'll do really well with that piece – no problem at all".

On the other hand, after being the under bidder and missing out by just one increment, the very same person could just as easily say "Did you see how much he's paid for that? – Crazy money, unbelievable, How the devil's he going to get his money back? I was just pushing him up." It is always the 'just pushing him up' bit that gets me, like it's really believable. I dare say the name of the game here is 'saving face'. I think some people, and not just dealers, imagine that the whole world is looking on whenever they 'lose out' to a rival. It isn't.

The reality is that irrespective of whether we are successful or not in our buying, there are many occasions when any of us can end up bidding right to our limit and even beyond. I dare say it might be different when we are competing for something that we desperately want to acquire and our limit can then be a little flexible. It is at all the other times, when the price gets to be right on the line and a feather placed on either side of the scale would make all the difference between buying and not.

When that is the case, why can't we just admit it and say "Yes that lot was OK, but frankly at that price I could take it or leave it, I wasn't too bothered either way." No, most of us don't seem to be able to do that. It seems we have to convince ourselves that, in winning, we had a heck of a good buy or, in losing, the other guy paid far too much. The simple truth is that at the end of the day, we all want to end up feeling good about ourselves.

It is only natural for most people who contact an auction house about selling items on their behalf, to ask when the next auction is. As an auctioneer, whenever you are asked this question you are fully aware that whatever date you say will be followed by an immediate assumption on the seller's part that their items will fall straight into it. You do not want to appear rude or flippant by saying that you can tell them when the next auction is right enough, but that this date might have no connection with when their own items are likely to be sold.

So you answer their question politely, and then qualify it by saying that time will be needed for cataloguing their lots, or other collections may already be in, or whatever. On one occasion I was speaking on the telephone to a gentleman with trains to sell and in answer to his question about the date of the next sale, I told him that the next auction was actually tomorrow. Before I had the chance to say any more, quick as a flash he asked, "What time will the items need delivering? – Oh, and by the way, will there be a catalogue?"

There is one topic even more popular amongst vendors than the next auction question. Now and again you will come across someone who has items to sell, but who professes to know absolutely nothing about auctions – never been to one, never seen one, knows absolutely nothing whatsoever. It is a strange thing, but in my experience, even when this is the case, you can bet your bottom dollar there is still one word they will know about – Reserve. You can guarantee it every time. It is uncanny. It is almost as though every young child is taught a word that will give his or her toys some protection in later life. As if it is something every infant learns when starting to talk. Like "Mummy", "Daddy" and then "Reserve".

The very word 'reserve' is one that is loved by nearly all sellers and hated by most buyers. The latter can sometimes have a fixation with reserves, which goes entirely beyond reason. In a sale we had some years ago, I cannot recall exactly what the items concerned were, but a string of consecutive almost identical train lots had been estimated very conservatively. The catalogues had just gone out and I took a call from a gentleman interested in these particular items. He asked me about them and I told him all I could. I added that they were there to be sold as he could see from the estimates, which were all set at £100 to £150. He said that he was determined to buy them and was prepared to go to about £500 each, but before doing that he would like to know if there were any reserves. You see, if you are not careful this reserve business can really play on the mind.

A reserve is very often confused with an estimate. There is a link, of course, as a buyer looking at the estimate knows that, barring any competition, a bid in that region should be enough to buy the lot. The setting of estimates is something most auction houses tend to be very careful with. As they are very well aware, the only safe estimate is a low one. In this way the buyer is attracted to the lot and when the item sells for that figure, or preferably (from the point of view of both the auction house and the vendor) goes sailing way over, the auction house is usually applauded for doing well. Not only can high estimates put many buyers off, but that person who just wanted those toys clearing out of the house can begin to have serious expectations once they see amounts of money printed against every lot.

I can recall picking up some trains from a man who was insistent that if we did not want them they were going down to the tip. There was no question about it, they were in the way, he needed the space and if I had not called to see him that day they were going to be dumped. After the catalogue, complete with estimates, landed on his doorstep, those self same trains that only a month or so earlier he had no interest whatsoever in were now seen in an entirely different light. He called me and asked whether we should think about some reserves – just to be on the safe side, you understand.

Then there is the matter of catalogue descriptions. Even though auction houses will always state that their descriptions are a matter of opinion only, if anything is sold that the buyer feels is not what he or she expected it to be, it is first the catalogue description and then the Conditions of Sale which are consulted.

I remember standing in Gilding's auction room in Market Harborough one day about twenty or more years ago. I must have gone there to buy something else in the sale, but a very pretty, small rocking horse, maybe late Victorian or early 1900s, took my eye. I had not spotted it in a brief glance through the catalogue, but I could clearly see that it was in superb condition and I thought it something that Marie might like. After deciding that I might go up to £250 or maybe a little more, I was more than pleased when the hammer came down at £160, which worked out to around £180 with the buyer's premium.

Back home, we stood it in the kitchen before considering whereabouts in the house it might fit best, when Marie and I both twigged the harsh reality at the same time. It was not old at all – the rocking horse was brand new. This was just before all those dark stained wooden items made to look old, like baby carriages, cribs, children's chairs and the rest began to flood in from the Continent and swamp all the large outdoor antiques fairs and every bric-a-brac stall and junk shop under the sun. Nowadays, these things seem to stand out like sore thumbs, but this must have been one of the first of these items to come over here and the possibility of it being made yesterday and only giving the appearance of age had not crossed my mind for a moment.

All I was left with then was that sickening feeling that you get when you realise you have bought a duffer. Immediately I thought of phoning John Gilding and taking the rocking horse straight back to the auction. I grabbed the catalogue to check the description, and very quickly realised that I had no case to put. There it was in the catalogue – the word 'style'. Not simply 'Victorian', but 'Victorian style'. The catalogue was quite accurate – I had simply failed to read it, or at least to read it properly. The rocking horse would have been fine if I had wanted something that merely *looked* old, but I didn't.

As we all know, once you buy anything that turns out not to be what you thought it was, getting rid of it can be the hardest thing. The rocking horse fiasco occurred shortly before Simon, Ellis and I had planned to travel down to the large outdoor autojumble, which was, and still is, held every September at the National Motor Museum near Beaulieu. There are hundreds of stalls here with all types of collectables for sale and many regular traders take caravans or tents to sleep in on site. We, however, in the company of many others who failed to appreciate the undoubted pleasures of camping, preferred the comforts of a nearby hotel.

We never went to Beaulieu with the expectation of selling very much; it was more just a fun weekend. We would take along a few toys and usually some pieces of old advertising and on this occasion, the decidedly out of favour rocking horse. I priced the animal at £225, hoping that we might be lucky and finish up with £200. We had already decided, however, that whatever price we achieved it would be selling and that 'Dobbin' would definitely not be rocking his way back home.

On the Friday, no sooner had we found our pitch and started setting out our stall than a Dutch dealer began to make a serious inspection of the rocking horse. Coming from the Netherlands of all places, where I had in the meantime discovered these things were actually made, I was waiting for him to say "I can get you plenty more of these, and a lot cheaper than this one." Instead, and without asking a single awkward or embarrassing question as to its age, he just said "I'll give you £150 for the horse." Chancing my arm in an effort to get my money back, I asked him to make it £180, he said £170 and as I was not going to risk it being unsold for one moment longer, I took his money.

No more than an hour or so later, Simon returned from a walk around the site only to report that out of all the hundreds of stalls and thousands of people at Beaulieu, the same Dutchman had a sales pitch exactly three stalls away from where we were stood. As he was going to be stuck there all weekend, what if he found out that the horse was new and then demanded his money back? Do we pack up right now and make a swift get-away while we have the chance? I had not pretended that the horse was old, so really there should have been nothing to worry about. Nevertheless, it was a fair bet that, exactly as I had done a couple of weeks earlier, he would simply have assumed it was.

Every time any of us went for a stroll around the stalls after that, we were always careful to give his pitch a wide berth – there was no sense in inviting trouble. Thankfully, he never came back and strangely enough, when we did manage to peer across from a safe distance, the rocking horse was nowhere to be seen. Perhaps he had sold it on again to yet another unsuspecting customer, or maybe after realising it was brand new he had simply smashed it up in frustration, or hidden it away out of embarrassment? Either way, as far as I was concerned, in selling that rocking horse I have never been happier to lose a tenner.

By Jim Whittaker

UNDER THE HAMMER

15

One parcel too many

For the first few years of running the Rugby auction, in order to keep the costs down to a minimum we didn't officially book the hall for the Friday, the day before the sale. Time was allowed for setting up on that day anyway, provided that there was no other function booked. Because the Friday was always clear of bookings this proved a sensible arrangement, as the additional expense could be avoided. We would set up as much as we needed to on the Friday and finish everything else the next morning.

After a while, when the venue became more popular, things began to change and quite often we would receive a call telling us that there was going to be a party or some other event on the Friday evening. Occasionally, we couldn't even get through the doors to do anything until 2am on the morning of the auction. Having to work through the night was a real killer. At least four or five hours would be needed to lay everything out and then we would be straight into a very busy auction day. At the end of a session like that, we were absolutely drained. There was one benefit though – getting to sleep the following night was never ever a problem.

Other than hiring the Benn Hall for the auction itself, we had never seriously considered taking on premises for the business, preferring always to work from home during hours to suit ourselves. The only time that staff were employed would be on the auction day itself. People such as Richard and David Small and Maurice and Margaret Darnes were a great help to us then, just as they are today. The downside of not having staff at other times was that we had to do everything ourselves – seeing clients with collections to sell, cataloguing, preparing accounts and doing the packing and sending of parcels for the absentee buyers.

Most people not directly involved with auctions would be surprised by just how much work there is to do both before and after the day of a sale. To the buyer in particular, everything appears to happen on sale day. I attended no end of auctions myself without ever giving a moment's thought to the preparation work that must have gone on before. Like all buyers, of course, there was neither reason nor desire to. I remember Bob Burgess from the Bassett-Lowke Society coming round to see us one day, when we had a pile of about forty large parcels stacked up in one corner. He could not believe that this small mountain of packages represented only about half the number needing to be wrapped and sent from the previous auction alone.

The dream scenario in running an auction, we always felt, would be to have a stack of commission bids on the books and then have a room full of people sat there outbidding every one. As far as we were concerned, the more items picked up and taken out of the door on the day the better. Whatever bulky and awkward lots were in the sale, you could guarantee these would be among the ones to attract pre-sale bids and it was amazing how often these large, unwieldy items needed to be packed and posted off somewhere. The difference in the amount of work required to handle lots selling on the books, compared with those sold in the room was considerable. Sending out the invoices, calculating the postage and (when the cheques finally came in) packing the parcels was a mammoth task.

The issue with parcels of course is that people naturally want their purchases sending immediately. If we didn't feel like packing parcels that particular day, that was tough luck; they had to be done. Any delay and people would soon be calling to ask whether their cheque had been received, when of course what they were really meaning was – where's my parcel? I remember quite a few occasions where people would call asking if their parcel had been sent yet, because they had posted a cheque to us as long as two or three days ago.

Running the business as a family concern, as we were, was becoming too much to cope with. We were rapidly getting to the point where either we expanded by taking on premises and staff, which was never our intention, or scaled the operation down just to have a life. That was around the time we had the approach from Vectis.

It was common knowledge that Roger Mazillius had sold his Vectis auction business eighteen months or so before to Bryan Goodall, a businessman from the Middlesbrough area. Bryan, a keen collector of Dinky and other diecast toys for many years, had been a frequent visitor to Roger's auction in Guildford and, following the sale of a business supplying food hampers, he had bought the Vectis operation and ventured into the world of auctions.

There was no doubt that Vectis was the leading auction house for diecast toys. They were finding things very different, however, on the train side, where in turn we were doing extremely well. Bryan had ambition for his company, but he could not see much of a change to the status quo, without taking some drastic action. John Morgan was with Vectis at the time and he phoned me to invite Ellis and myself out

Barry Potter Auctions

Collectable Toys and Trains

Saturday 19th February 2000
The Benn Hall, Rugby

Viewing 9am - 11am   Auction starts 11am
Catalogue £7   Admits Two

A new style of Rugby catalogue

for lunch. It was then he told us that Vectis were interested in buying our auction business. After that first meeting we were keen enough to meet again, this time with him and Bryan together and we got on well, but being uncertain as to whether this was really the best move for us, we did nothing further.

A few months passed and we came to the clear conclusion that we didn't want to go on working all hours indefinitely. We had not set out to sell the business, nor did we need to. On the other hand, we could not really see ourselves taking on the premises and staff that sooner or later would most certainly be needed. In view of this, we felt that perhaps we should reconsider. I called Bryan, we met up again and shortly afterwards, which was early in 1998, agreed a deal to sell the auction business to Vectis.

Bryan was putting a good team together at Thornaby, with Vicky Screen (whose married name is now Weall) as General Manager. The cataloguing team included David Nathan, an old friend I had known for years and who had moved north to join the company. David had been on the toy scene for a long time as both a collector and a dealer and was at one time Editor of the Hornby Railway Collectors' Association magazine. Before David began working full time with toys, one of his career moves was into selling insurance and just after I became self employed he must have viewed me as a red hot prospect, because after some very smooth talking he managed to rope me into a policy. That was more than twenty-five years ago – and I am still trying to figure out a way of getting my own back.

Also on the cataloguing team at Vectis were Andrew Reed, Julian Royse and Ian Dilley, whilst Debbie Cockerill and others were looking after the administration side. Since then Mike Delaney has joined the team to catalogue the 0 gauge and larger trains and Michael Bond the 00 gauge. With even more specialists on the cataloguing side such as Peter Rumsey, Simon Clark, Kathy Taylor and David

Bowers and many others involved with photography, catalogue design and administration, there are currently more than thirty people employed by Vectis Auctions. Looking back, it was a real surprise to many people that we had sold our auction business and quite a few wondered whether we had been right to do so. We, however, had no doubts.

The arrangement was for Ellis and myself to be involved for a period of two years, during which time the administration side would be moved to the Vectis offices in Thornaby, Stockton-on-Tees. There were no plans to change the format of the Rugby auction; it was working well enough and would remain exactly as it was. As far as we were concerned, in addition to the auctioneering and for the two-year period of the agreement we would look after the cataloguing side of things. Life immediately became so much easier. All the paperwork, which without a computer accounts system we had found so time-consuming, and the packing of the parcels was now handled at Thornaby.

Undoubtedly the best collection we have dealt with at Rugby to date was that belonging to the late Al Markham. This came up about eighteen months after we sold the business to Vectis.

Living in Toronto, Al, just like his father John before him, had been a collector of trains all his life. I was familiar with his name and knew that he had been a very good friend of John Ridley for years. It was Peter Aziz though, another friend of Al's and also from Toronto, who contacted me concerning the collection. Peter felt that it would be useful if Ellis and I came out to see everything whilst it was still in place at Mr. Markham's house, and so we booked the necessary flights and hotel.

The collection filled two large basement rooms and when first we came down the steps it was a sight to behold. There was a layout in both rooms and many more trains and toys on shelves around the walls. There was much to take in and we spent about two or three days going through it all.

There cannot be too many people in the train world with the surname of Aziz, and Peter is a cousin of Paul, who, as he was living at that time in Connecticut, took the opportunity of coming over to see the collection whilst we were there. We now had double Aziz expertise on the case. Paul's speciality has always been Bassett-Lowke and there was certainly plenty there for him to run the slide rule over. It was a lot of fun looking at everything and discussing things together. Peter was a great help to us in Canada. Al Markham and he had been very close and he simply wanted the best outcome for his friend's collection. Peter invited us over to his house to meet his wife Mary and young son Cameron, and we had a great time.

Al's wishes had been for the proceeds from the eventual sale of his collection to be donated to various Canadian charities. As he had been a widower and there were no children, the disposal was overseen by a nephew and niece. They knew little of the collecting world, but were doing a more than thorough job in talking not just to us but to representatives from a number of different auction houses. We very much wanted to win the right to sell the collection, so we had to tread carefully.

There was a high proportion of European trains, including Hornby, Bassett-Lowke, Märklin and Bing as well as American models by Lionel, American Flyer, Ives etc. The collection also included a large number of tinplate toys, especially boats. We knew that the American trains would sell in England, but as we had a feeling that the family might perceive them doing a little better in the United States, we tailored our proposal accordingly. Our pitch to Al's nephew and niece was that we would deal with all the European trains and the tinplate toys, whilst the American trains should be sold in the USA. They had even more auction people to see after us, so things were not certain by any means, but in the end we were very pleased when they decided to go ahead with our proposal. Ralston's was the auction house selected to sell the American trains.

Our contract with the family specified that we would handle the packing and shipping of the collection back to England. Vicky Weall and David Nathan went over together and, with help from Peter Aziz, spent the best part of a week carefully packing everything in tissue, bubble wrap and boxes, before the whole lot was delivered to England by container.

The intention all along, if we managed to secure the collection, had been to hold a special Markham Collection auction at Rail 2000 – a massive event planned to celebrate the 175th anniversary of the opening of the Stockton and Darlington Railway. This was to be a high profile occasion planned for the August Bank Holiday weekend in 2000, and many thousands of visitors were expected. Devised around the prospect of a huge cavalcade of steam locomotives, it promised to be even more impressive than the Shildon festival of twenty-five years before.

The auction was to be held in a locomotive shed in Darlington, the very place where the new A1 steam locomotive 'Tornado' was being built. We had much riding on Rail 2000. In addition to the auction, we had been asked to organise toy collectors fairs at each of four planned sites along the route and a large amount of our time and money was spent on designing and printing brochures. We had many trips up to Darlington and discussions with the Rail 2000 management team, and the whole event was an exciting prospect.

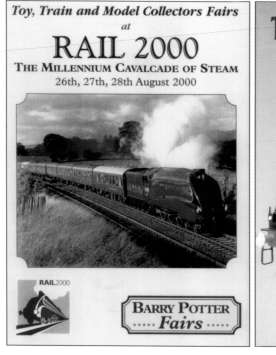

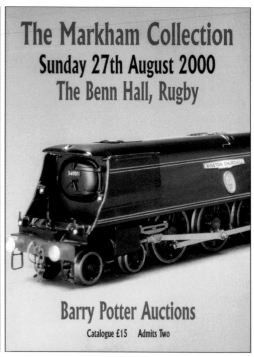

The biggest train event that never took place   The Markham Collection catalogue

The meetings were all very positive at first, but after a while it began to concern us that things might not be going as well as had been anticipated. Everything was in place at our end, but as the months leading up to the event were passing by, little seemed to be happening on site. Our worst fears were realised when we discovered that the management team had run out of money, no further sponsors could be found, and the whole project had been cancelled. By this time we had already delivered the text for the Markham auction catalogues to the printers. Luckily, we managed in the nick of time to reschedule the sale to Rugby and have the catalogues altered accordingly.

The Markham Collection auction was held at the Benn Hall in Rugby on Sunday 27th August 2000, the very date originally scheduled for Rail 2000 and our first ever Sunday sale. Al Markham's nephew and niece came over specially, as did a number of American collectors. Some of the sale highlights included a Bassett-Lowke 0 gauge model of Sir Winston Churchill's funeral train which made £12,000, a Märklin gauge 1 Hospital Coach £4,100 and an 0 gauge Bassett-Lowke 'Coronation' £8,500. An 0 gauge Märklin Station complex made £10,000, a Märklin gauge 1 'Stephenson' locomotive £6,000 and a Märklin model of the 'Hindenburg' airship sold for £11,500. The large tinplate ships also attracted much interest, as did other more usual items such as Hornby 0 gauge and Dublo, Wrenn and Triang Minics.

This sale contained the best of Al Markham's collection, with his lesser items all selling through our other auctions. In total, I believe the Markham collection realised around half a million pounds. All cataloguing after that date was carried out at Thornaby, this being the last auction that Ellis and I were to handle from start to finish.

At the end of the two-year period with Vectis, Ellis and I were pleased with the way that things had worked out and were keen to remain involved. A contract was agreed for us to continue as Auctioneers and Consultants and to deal with clients having collections to sell. When we first joined Vectis, their auctions were held in the Royal National Hotel in London and then for a few years in Buckingham. From January 2004, it was decided that all auctions, except for those in Rugby, would be held at the Vectis head offices in Thornaby. A special auction room was built, together with a separate viewing room large enough to display all the lots, for what had now expanded to a regular three-day sale and later, towards the end of 2006, even to four days every month.

The number of Vectis auctions now is staggering. As well as diecast toys and trains, there are special sales of lead and plastic figures, tinplate toys and dolls and teddy bears. With the Rugby and Thornaby sales added together, there are currently no less than sixty days of Vectis auctions scheduled each year. Towards the end of 2005, after a larger number of consignments than usual had been logged in, the scheduled three day auction at Thornaby became five and with a Saturday train sale following, there were to be six auctions within ten days.

From Dinky Toys to Dan Dare guns to Joanna Lumley's original Spitting Image puppet, in a ten day period that December, Ellis and I put the hammer down on more than 4800 lots, adding up to more than half a million pounds worth of toys sold. I don't know how many parcels needed packing after that, but we would have been struggling to manage them in our double garage, that is for sure.

One recent development has been the live bidding on the internet. Every Vectis sale is now linked through to ebay, allowing live on-line bidding as the auction is conducted in the room. The whole catalogue can be viewed on ebay lot by lot, up to three weeks before the day of the auction. Those not wishing to participate in the live bidding, but who have viewed the sale on the ebay site, can leave absentee bids on line, which will automatically be brought into play once the auction is underway.

As far as the live bidding itself is concerned, there are no cameras in the auction room, but a computer keyboard operator in the saleroom continually updates the on-line bidders with the progress of the sale. Vital to this working correctly is the auctioneer's use of fixed bidding increments, matching ones already programmed into the computer. The fixed increments allow the keyboard operator to keep on-line bidders informed of the progress of the lot and what the next increment is, should they choose to make a bid. When a bid comes in on-line, an assistant to the operator signals to the auctioneer, enabling him to take bids from the internet against bidders in the room, on the telephone, or others also on the internet.

As an auctioneer, the on-line bidding can certainly keep you on your toes. Quite often when a lot comes up which everyone wants, there can be bids on the book, numerous bids in the room, bidders on maybe five or six different telephones and then bids coming through the internet. At times like that, when things are really buzzing and bids are flying in from all directions, you almost expect the clock on the wall to start twitching.

As users of ebay will know, one feature which is promoted very strongly on that system is entitled 'Ask the Seller a Question'. For potential purchasers of course, this can be a very useful facility, as there could well be legitimate and very sensible questions to be asked. To keep the number of potential questions down to a minimum, the cataloguing team at Vectis, especially on the diecast side which is probably that section of the business attracting most internet interest, try their best to pre-empt most queries by the quality of their catalogue descriptions.

Nevertheless, there is no doubt that for some people an invitation to ask a question about anything under the sun can be akin to showing a sunflower to a bee or perhaps even a red rag to a bull. Consequently, those members of staff who look after the internet enquiries at Vectis with admirable patience inevitably have a huge stack of questions to wade through and answer before every sale. Whether the question is about the particular type of wheels on a Dinky car, the colour of the interior, or whatever, anyone doing that job for a long spell can quickly become an expert on most toys. In fact, there are some questions they are able to answer without even needing to go off and look at the models. These include such memorable ones as "Your description says they are all Poor to Fair – Are there any that are Mint?" or "What colour is the white Mercedes?"

This new way of bidding does bring the auction within reach of anyone anywhere in the world and as such, it must attract more buyers. As useful as it is, however, for many people, there will never be anything to beat actually being there in the room. It is very easy to think that with all the publicity surrounding certain items selling for high prices, that everything at auction is expensive, which of course is nonsense. There are bargains at every sale and usually it is the people who have made the effort to go along on the day who benefit.

Rare and especially top condition items in a well-known and popular series will usually be contested strongly, and when that happens it is all down to how comfortable you feel about the price. For many serious collectors, when an item comes along which they really want, the main concern is often acquiring it and the price required to do so may be secondary. Whether you are a collector or a dealer, there is a strong argument for buying items high on everyone's desirability list. You can reason that, with something a lot of people would like to own, no matter how high the price might seem at the time, there is the thought that should you at some stage wish to sell, there will probably be someone out there prepared to buy.

The real bargains though are often to be found amongst the off beat and unusual lots. These are the items outside the collecting interest of most bidders and they can sometimes be bought quite cheaply. I suppose that if you are a dealer, the trick is to buy in a place and at a time when few people are interested and then sell when the right buyers are paying attention. You see, what could be easier than that?

In one sense the life of our family has now almost come full circle. After moving from the Leeds area in 1977, it is there that Ellis and I now stay when we go up to Thornaby for the four-day sales.

Much of Leeds has changed almost out of all recognition since we lived in the area. Having always being a city of some character, much of the centre has now been transformed. There are many superb restaurants (we should know, we have tried most of them) and fancy shops such as Harvey Nichols, although it has always been the best town I have known for shopping anyway.

Ellis has an apartment in Leeds. It overlooks Leeds General Infirmary where he was born and also the Civic Hall where I used to work. Just below is Brown's restaurant, in the shell of what was once the Leeds Permanent Building Society where Marie and I took out our first mortgage. For me, it is a very nice but still slightly strange feeling going back to the town I used to know so well.

By Jim Whittaker

COLLECTING

16

The thrill of the chase

We all collect in different ways. Some of us choose to keep only those items we find the most appealing regardless of make, and that has always been my way. I have never been one for concentrating on one area for too long, which is a trait I know to be long acquired, as I clearly remember it being an observation from one of my teachers at school.

For many others, however, once they embark on a favoured theme or make, no stone is left unturned until every example and variation is owned. As far as trains are concerned, people such as Chris and Julie Graebe with Hornby 0 gauge, Bob Field with Hornby Dublo and David O'Brien with Trix will derive great pleasure collecting and researching their subjects in depth. Even though collecting one make or brand with that level of intensity has never been my approach, I can appreciate its attraction.

Collecting in that way, as they and many others like them do, is never ending. There are forever new finds to be made and more research to be done into different aspects. This type of collecting dedication can also come in very handy, for if there is anything you need to know on these subjects – if these guys don't know the answers, no one does.

The real joy for so many people is the act of collecting itself; the building of a collection as it were, even more than the end product. Quite often, particularly when someone has been collecting within a series – one for which they can see a definite completion to – after finally tracking down those last few elusive items and ticking all the boxes, rather than a feeling of contentment, there can be a distinct sense of anticlimax. The collection is out on display looking wonderful and yet all those elements they have enjoyed the most – the searching out of all these toys, the haggling and banter with the dealers, the bidding at auction have all suddenly finished. The real thrill, they realise, was actually in the chase itself. What happens next – Where do they go from there?

Although it so often does, it should really come as no surprise to find someone suddenly intent on selling a collection they have spent years enthusiastically putting together. Unfortunately, this is sometimes viewed as a sign of someone being casual or superficial, as though the person concerned could not have been collecting seriously from the outset. This is nonsense. We should simply accept the fact that the real pleasure for so many people is the seeking out of these toys and trains and of putting that collection together in the first place.

Many of us have ever-changing and evolving tastes. I know I do. Selling a collection and starting again in another direction is not uncommon. In fact it is not always a change of direction. I have known more than a few people, only a year or even less after selling their collection, begin all over again. Perhaps with a slight change of emphasis, but otherwise along exactly the same route as before. Whatever we choose to do, whether it is to collect indefinitely along the same vein or to chop and change every now and again, there is no doubt that so much of the fun can most definitely be in the search.

Whilst we all enjoy looking for and acquiring items, there is one group of people most decidedly not inclined to sell up and steer the good ship 'Collecting' along a different course. These are the people I would affectionately refer to as the Old School Collectors. These, mainly older people and very often train enthusiasts who managed to put the bulk of their collections together in the early days, have a quite different approach to collecting than we more recent upstarts. The true measure of an old school collector I would suggest is that the very idea of anything being sold goes completely against the grain. An odd item might be sacrificed if a similar one in better condition is found but, that apart, once an item is in the display case or on the layout, there it must remain until last orders are called.

Then there are those people whom the dealers and auction houses like to see best of all. These are the ones welcomed with open arms – the high rollers. Those comfortably to very well off collectors, the ones who can afford to keep on buying whatever takes their fancy without worrying for one moment about the expense. They might not always want to admit it, but they have the funds to buy the best items and will build a collection accordingly. Even though these collectors may be in the wealthy bracket, as most of them will not have arrived there by being reckless with money, they are not likely to change that philosophy simply to buy toys and trains. They might operate on a higher budget than many other collectors, but in their own way they are just as careful over what is purchased.

A wealthy collector might well want to acquire the best condition or scarcest items available, but no matter how ambitious their spending plan might be or how many items they might want to own, they are no different from the rest of us when it comes to one fundamental principle. Whatever price any of us are considering paying for any toy or train, even at the highest level, we will still want to feel that it represents as much value in the market place as we can judge it to have.

You might imagine that some people in the high roller category would be collecting purely for investment. In my view, however, any such assumptions are a complete fallacy. In my experience, there is simply no such person as one who collects toys or trains for investment alone. Certainly there are many who will view their growing collection as a future nest egg and will hope that values continue to rise, but I do not believe anyone would cite that as the sole reason for their having started collecting in the first place.

That initial collecting spark might come from a memory of these things from childhood, either what they had back then, or as in my case, didn't have but wanted. Just as likely, though, is that the collecting will kick off when someone comes across an odd toy or some trains for the first time, and simply finds the idea of keeping whatever it is appealing. We all collect these things because we like them – anything else along the way is simply a bonus.

After reading the earlier chapters, you will not be surprised if I suggest that the three main places from which to buy toys and trains are, in strictly unbiased alphabetical order, auctions, dealers and toy fairs. As a possible fourth, you can always take your life in your hands and click on to the internet, but you will have to be very lucky to succeed anywhere else. When it comes to dealers in antiques or in general collectables, most tend to view anything in the toy and train line through rose-tinted spectacles. If they do have anything for sale, the chances are the price will be high, and sometimes absurdly so. In fact the likelihood of finding anything worth buying at that Sunday morning institution the car boot sale, or even at a decent antiques fair these days is slim indeed.

This is hardly surprising when you stop to think about it. As the amount of old toys and trains lying undiscovered in attics, or in any place where they are not treasured, begins to dry up, the less likely these things are to turn up in non-specialist areas. Once anything becomes the property of a collector, from that point forward, whoever is responsible for their ultimate selling will naturally want them to appear in a place where people are going to take notice. Apart from the internet minefield, this means auctions, in the hands of dealers or toy fairs.

Collecting Clubs and Associations are a big help to many collectors. Firstly, they can provide a forum for members to discuss or find out more about models through newsletters and magazines. More importantly, with the arranging of collecting events and, in the case of trains, running events, they bring like-minded people together and it is this social side of the hobby that so many enjoy.

Not being a collector of diecast models, I am unfamiliar with the detailed workings of their clubs, but the Maidenhead Static Model Club and the Coventry Diecast Model Club are perhaps the two best known. They have regular meetings and sometimes even arrange trips to toy events overseas.

As far as trains are concerned, the three largest collecting associations in Britain are the Hornby Railway Collectors' Association, the Train Collectors' Society and the Bassett-Lowke Society. Common to all of them, is the production of a part-colour monthly magazine for members.

The largest of the three associations is the HRCA with around three thousand members. The HRCA publishes a very comprehensive directory of spare parts and suppliers and members arrange regular get-togethers in different parts of the country, usually with working layouts and sales tables. Deserving of a special mention here is the late John Kitchen, who served in the roles of Chairman and President so well for more than thirty years. I have no idea how many get-togethers, AGMs or auctions John presided over in that time; perhaps even he had lost count. One thing is for sure. The prices of Hornby trains will have been a lot different back in 1969 when the HRCA was founded by the two Peters, Gomm and Randall. The HRCA's present Chairman, David Embling, is currently working hard to ensure that the Association remains strong and healthy.

The Train Collectors' Society with David Ramsey as Chairman and Pat Hammond who recently succeeded Jeff Carpenter as Editor of the monthly TCS magazine is another very well run organisation. The TCS arranges various events for members, including the AGM at Biggleswade and an annual Model Railway and Toy Train Exhibition with sales tables and no less than 30 various railway layouts on display at Sandy in Bedfordshire.

The Bassett-Lowke Society Chairman is Mike Green, who does an excellent job keeping a very enthusiastic band of collectors in check. Kate Chester-Lamb is responsible for the monthly Lowko News, transforming it from a simple black and

The Bassett-Lowke Society event at Tewin with layouts in both gauges 1 and 0

white newsletter to a very readable magazine full of photographs. Just as the HRCA is custodian of many original Meccano Ltd documents, the Society looks after an archive of various historic Bassett-Lowke records. Regular meetings and get-togethers for members are held, including an occasional very elaborate affair at the National Railway Museum in York.

It was the social side of the hobby that was uppermost in the minds of John Neale and myself when together we first arranged a rather different type of train event. The idea was hatched following a very pleasant lunch for a group of fellow train collectors at Kilworth House Hotel in Leicestershire – most things look possible of course after a glass or two of wine.

It would be nice, we thought, if a lunch and get-together could be arranged on a large scale using the splendid Victorian Orangery at Kilworth, which along with the rest of the property had recently been restored and converted from a private mansion to a luxury country house hotel. As it was something we wanted to do personally and would be non-profit making, because the hotel management were very keen on charity work, it would be fitting, we thought, if the event could also help with their fund raising.

The first 'Trains at Kilworth House' took place on Sunday 6th November 2005. A three-course lunch for 150 collectors was served in the Orangery and there were twenty sales tables packed with trains from well-known dealers and collectors in two side rooms. The guest speakers were themselves well-known collectors and authors of train collecting books – Chris and Julie Graebe and Michael Foster – and all three were brilliant. Chris and Julie came on first as a double act and entertained everyone no end with their collecting stories, especially some of the prices paid 25 years back. They claimed it was the first time they had given such a talk, but observing their polished delivery, you would not have thought so.

Michael's talk was equally entertaining, even though his wife Yvonne did appear a little worried at times over what he might have been about to say next. The talk passed without anything unduly risqué being said, however, (maybe she had pre-warned him) and at the end he proposed a toast to friendship, which as he so rightly said, is such a lovely part of collecting.

Chris and Julie Graebe giving their talk at Kilworth House Hotel,
November 2005

After the talks, there was an auction from which all commission raised was given to charity. Ace Trains kindly donated a special A4 locomotive named 'W.J. Bassett-Lowke', which alone made £1,035 for the cause and in total the auction contributed a tidy £8,200 towards Breast Cancer Research. Afterwards, John Neale, his wife Diana, Marie and I agreed that the event had been a great success and we lost no time in arranging another at Kilworth House for the following year.

That event went ahead on Sunday 22nd October 2006 and the charity to benefit was the Motor Neurone Disease Association. David Pressland was guest speaker and he gave us a thought-provoking talk about the early evolution of tinplate toy trains, illustrated by a number of special items from his collection. David has always been known as a collector of tin toys, but the trains he brought along by companies such as Lutz dating from as early as the 1850s and including a wonderfully detailed and fragile Der Adler set were spectacular. Immediately after his talk many of the guests were quickly out of their seats for a closer inspection of the trains.

Again, the auction went very well, with Ace Trains donating another locomotive – this time a BR blue A3 'Trigo' of which only three were made – contributing £1,150 to the charity. We had not expected the final figure to reach, let alone beat, that of the previous year and it was great to see the money raised to help fight Motor Neurone Disease total £10,288.

Among the lots sold in the auction was one donated by the hotel, giving two people an overnight stay, dinner with champagne, wine and luxury chocolates which raised around £300. This lot had caught the eye of my good friend Maurice Darnes, who

David Pressland giving his talk on early trains, October 2006 (photo by David Barzilay)

John Neale and I presenting the cheque for £10,288 for The Motor Neurone Disease
Association to Celia Mackay, owner of Kilworth House Hotel

obviously wanted to give his wife Margaret a special treat. It remains a mystery as
to just how he managed to get Margaret out of the Orangery at the precise time the
lot was coming up, but while she was distracted, he bid and bought it – obviously
a true romantic.

Graham de Chastelain, every month or so in the summer, enjoys nothing better than
inviting about twenty friends over to his house for a 'Running Day'. Not a lengthy
session of vigorous exercise of course, but an opportunity for fellow train buffs to
let their wares loose on Graham's garden railway. Just how many come and from
how far afield clearly shows how much they enjoy it. Mike Green, Peter Beale,
Joyce and Maurice Shutler, Peter O'Kane, John Ingram, Peter Gomm, Keith Bone,
Stewart Bean, David Ramsey, Mike King, Andrew Hurley and Douglas Baldock
are among the regulars.

Living on the far side of Northamptonshire, Graham's house is a mere twenty miles
or so from mine, unlike George Johnson and Kevin Ludlow who come down from
Bolton and Paul Aziz who drives up the motorway from London. Graham usually
lays on the food, everyone else the drink and the day is a pleasant mix of trains and
chat. Sat in the garden, the sun shining, a train winding round the track, and not
forgetting a glass of wine in the hand, is not a bad way to spend an afternoon. This
train business can be hard work.

COLLECTING

17

How rare is rare?

Back in the 1970s when I started, as far as most collectors were concerned, whatever their particular collecting field was, their likely objective would be to own an example of every variation in it. Looking for Dinky Toy lorries, say, they would want one of each cab type and every colour combination. What are the axles like? Does this one have the smooth hubs or the ridged ones? Likewise with trains. It would be the colours and running numbers, or maybe this one has fluted coupling rods, this engine has its wheels just pressed on the axle not screwed.

Back then, if something came along in brand new, ex-shop stock condition with the original box, that would be a nice bonus, but the main criterion would still be – is it an example I haven't got? The whole emphasis then for most people was on variation, as it still is with many of the older collectors and indeed with specialists in a particular toy or train maker today.

Nowadays, as a result of prices increasing rapidly during the 1980s and 1990s and more collectors feeling obliged to consider their options a little more carefully before plunging in to buy, for many people an item's condition is not just king, it can be everything. Whereas at one time the most desirable element was always rarity, far more often now it is simply condition.

The rarer items are still highly desired of course and it is impossible to make a direct comparison on a like for like basis, rarity against condition. Nevertheless, if faced with the choice of a moderately hard to find item in average condition and a common one which is mint, many more collectors now, especially the newer ones, would plump for the latter. Best of all is a hard to find item that everyone wants in perfect condition. Have one of those and you can really call the shots.

Having the accent fully on condition for some time now has had its effect on prices. In the two areas of interest to most people, that is diecast toys and trains, not unexpectedly perhaps, the perfect and near to perfect items are selling for very high prices. Conversely, those at the very bottom of the condition scale, the ones complete but tatty are also in demand often as restoration projects. The prices tending to stagnate or even fall are for items in that middle band, the toys and trains in average condition – the ones many collectors would deem not quite good enough to keep and yet far too nice to restore. If anything, as time goes by and more collectors become fussier over condition, the gulf between values for these average items and their perfect cousins is getting wider.

The current flatness of prices in the middle ground of average to good condition is something of a boon to those toy train collectors who also run trains. Many people for example find Hornby Dublo 3-rail so much more fun to use than the marvellously detailed products made today. It is a similar story with diecast. Those collectors who are not unduly obsessive about condition, but who are happy to have items in that middle condition band are at present enjoying buying at prices very often no higher than would have been paid ten or fifteen years ago.

Television and film of course dominate the age we live in and anything related to programmes and characters we know on the screen is avidly collected. Indeed, much of today's brand new diecast toy production has a TV or film connection. Mostly it relates to the old well-loved favourites, although nowadays any newly released film or TV programme which takes off can have its own toys in the shops in no time.

This surge in interest for TV and film related toys has prompted collectors to look afresh at items from the 1960s and 1970s by Dinky and especially by Corgi. All of these toys such as James Bond cars, Batman, The Saint or The Avengers have forever been popular, but the interest in them at present is huge. The same can be said for Star Wars toys. You might imagine that the newly produced figures and models would have an adverse affect on the value of the old ones, but you would be wrong. Ironically, the vast production of no end of brand new toys relating to these science fiction classics seems to stir the desire for their original 1970s equivalents even more.

Two words often confused with each other when it comes to collecting are 'rare' and 'desirable'. In some people's minds, anything considered to be rare must also be valuable; it has to be worth money. Not so – you could have what in reality might be the rarest toy in the world, a simple item produced in a factory somewhere as a one-off, but if no one was interested, it could be worth next to nothing.

When it comes to most toys and trains, rarity in isolation is not enough and no guarantee of desirability and therefore of value. As far as diecast toys and most trains are concerned, the rarity must be related to something that collectors can identify with in the first place. Fundamentally though, the item must have been produced by, or linked in some way, to a strongly collected maker.

If you stumbled across a diecast toy car without a maker's mark that no one in the collecting world had ever seen before, it would very probably generate enough interest and novelty value to be worth a good few pounds – if you were lucky maybe even a hundred. If, however, an equally unfamiliar item was stamped 'Made by Meccano Ltd' or 'Märklin' it could fetch thousands.

After the importance of condition, the most desirable train or diecast items are inevitably the hardest to find or most attractive in an avidly collected series by a well-known maker. For so many collectors, the products from Meccano Ltd, mostly Dinky Toys, Hornby Dublo and Hornby 0 gauge trains are the perennial favourites. That company's entire production exuded quality, which is why their toys are so wanted today. Indeed, almost every item originating from Meccano's now defunct Liverpool factory is now desirable to collectors.

Now and again someone will say to me "Barry! Just the man. I've got something very rare to show you. I've never seen one before – it could be good for the auction." Of course it might well be something good and I am always as keen as mustard to look. On the other hand, after seeing so many 'rare' items, including ones

Jim Whittaker's Lowry style impression of the Meccano factory

so offbeat and ones we have struggled in the past to find a buyer for, I am equally prepared for disappointment.

Some collectors have the notion that, although their interest lies in the very toys and trains most people would identify with, there is this whole horde of others out there searching for the obscure, when in reality almost everyone wants the same. This is why, if the item in question is a slightly quirky toy or train and not something produced by a well known maker, unless it happens to be a very early piece, the chances of it being desirable are slim. In such situations it is very tempting to say "Thank you, but please don't worry about anything being rare. Just show me a regular toy or train everyone knows, something in nice condition, something people will actually want."

After saying all that, when it comes to tin toys, things can be very different. Unlike diecast and all but the earliest trains, as far as tin toys are concerned, an item's visual appeal would be enough to make people want it. For me, and I know I would echo the thoughts of most other tin toy collectors here, the appearance is the main issue. This, together with the condition and the price are the only three factors that would determine whether or not most collectors would want to own a particular tin toy.

Because the need to associate something with a maker's name is so crucial in the train and diecast field, this same yardstick is often wrongly carried over and applied to tin toys. So many people, after coming across a tin toy, feel obliged to immediately embark upon a never ending, no stone left unturned quest to discover the maker. The truth is, that unless the toy in question is an extremely early piece, or there is a chance that it might be linked to Märklin, frankly, other than satisfying someone's curiosity, knowing the maker is of little importance. It is not as if being able to assign a maker's name to the toy will affect its value. It hardly ever will – identifying the maker is purely academic. With a tin toy, the item will almost invariably be judged on its individual merits, regardless of make.

Now and again you will overhear a discussion "I think it's Distler", "No, I'm pretty sure it's Karl Bub", "No, look I'm sure it's Distler, mind you the wheels do look a bit like Bing." With some people, it is almost as though, if you can put a maker's name to it, you have passed a test, a confirmation among your mates of your superior knowledge – like being awarded a Scouting badge for 'Tin Toy Identification'.

I remember a man taking a shine to a tin car I once had. I told him it was Japanese. "Blimey! You're clever!" he said, looking at me a bit quizzically "How do you know that? How do you know it's Japanese?" Resisting the temptation to bask in any more of this ill-earned praise, I pointed inside the back window and said "Look – see what it says – Made in Japan." There are times when you just have to know your stuff.

COLLECTING

18

For *you*, Sir

I am not certain when it was that I first thought of myself as a collector. Starting to buy Hornby Dublo in 1971, my initial intention was to have the trains I had always wanted as a boy and then to build a model railway with them. The realisation that I was actually collecting these things was more gradual, and began to take shape only after moving down to the Midlands and becoming aware of the whole collecting scene and just how many other people were out there with the same interests.

Trains were where I started, although my collection of them now is quite small. After once having a room full of 0 gauge and gauge 1, it pleases me more at present to keep only a few special favourites. Tin toys have been an interest for a long time and right now I am equally keen on them. As far as diecast goes, I have always liked the way the 1950s and 1960s Dinky and Corgi Toys reflect the period so well, not only the models themselves but equally the packaging. After saying that, I have never felt the desire to put a collection of them together, nor have I ever been keen to collect lead soldiers, although I do have a few civilian lead figures and sets.

In the loft of our house in Yorkshire I had a reasonable layout of Hornby Dublo trains. My son Simon and I built it together and for a few years it was good fun. As time passed, however, and as pulling the loft ladder down and climbing up into the roof space seemed more trouble than say just walking into another room and switching the trains on would have been, the layout was not being used very much.

Not long after moving to Market Harborough, 0 gauge began to have more appeal for me and I very soon had a sizeable layout around a bedroom, seventeen feet by twelve. The track-work was Bassett-Lowke as were some of the buildings and accessories, the rest being mainly Hornby. The trains were mostly electric, except that now and again it was fun to have a live steamer like a Bassett-Lowke Mogul running around. Although the layout remained in place for perhaps two or three years, after the first six months or so the trains were not actually running that often. As I was buying more and more trains, the layout became merely somewhere on which to stand them.

Ultimately, I came to realise that my interest had developed more into simply collecting trains rather than running them. I know a lot of people enjoy building layouts, either for themselves or for exhibitions, which is fine and I am pleased they do. For my part, I enjoy seeing trains running, but after a few minutes I have had enough. I am just as happy to look at models on display and to chat to collectors about various aspects as I am to see them moving about. Once the layout was dismantled I kept my collection in the same room, although now in static mode on shelves and in cases around the walls.

We all need something to inspire our collecting and I think that, in my case, two very large books helped a lot. One was 'A Century of Model Trains' by Allen Levy and the other 'The Art of the Tin Toy' by David Pressland. Allen's book was great. It gave me a real flavour of what had been produced by the famous makers, and therefore, what might be out there to find. Looking through it for the first time, I would have been only a little way into the train world and pictured here were far more varieties than I was aware of.

The anticipation that at some point there might be a chance of discovering these things was exciting. In the early days I remember someone telephoning about an 0 gauge locomotive he had which was named 'Stephenson'. After studying a photograph in the book showing two different examples by Märklin, it was fun, armed with the knowledge of what these things should look like, to go out as the most recent 'Märklin expert' in town, buy the engine and then compare it with the two illustrated.

There are few things in life quite as potent as enthusiasm. Occasionally, however, if you are not careful it can run out of control. After acquiring the 'Stephenson', I was fired up to try to buy a gauge 1 version of the same engine to go with it. The locomotive was coming up in a Christie's auction at the Brighton Engineerium in the September of 1980. The engine was in truly superb condition, which served only to attract the attention of every Märklin enthusiast on the planet and inspire me to bid considerably more than was planned. Actually, that is not strictly true, as no exact price was decided on beforehand, which is always the most dangerous strategy, or lack of it, to take into any auction.

Patrick Lindsay was the auctioneer that day and when his hammer finally came down at £3,500, I distinctly remember him pointing towards me and announcing "For *you,* Sir". In singling me out publicly in that way, it was almost as though he was insuring against my having second thoughts and making a swift exit out of the back door. With the buyer's premium added on there was little change from four grand, and selling myself the decision to buy became a little harder that day than usual. Allen's book was to blame. There is no doubt about it.

David Pressland's book was even more of a revelation and opened the door on a world that, until then, I never knew existed. Right from the superbly printed outer board covers adorned with great toys, all the way through the toy battleships, liners, cars, aeroplanes and a multitude of novelty toys, these were things for the most part I had never seen. Such is the scarcity of some, even after nearly thirty years of looking there are many I still have not set eyes on. That is the nice thing though about tin toys – it really doesn't matter that you have not seen most things – with so many varieties you are simply not expected to.

With tinplate it can be surprising just how often you will come across a toy, only to realise that it is an example you are looking at for the very first time. We all have fun trying to discover, but none of us will ever fully know what was made and what might be out there still to find.

David Pressland is a collector like few others. He began with Dinky Toys as a boy in the 1950s and gradually as he discovered tin toys, they became his passion. A real authority on tinplate, he has now written three books on the subject including one on a particular speciality of his, Penny Toys. In recent years he has become very interested in early horse drawn toys by companies like Märklin, Lutz and Übelacker. These are extremely rare toys of course, for which you have to know where to look. With items such as these, where on earth do you start? It is hard to imagine for example anyone having much success walking into their local charity shop and asking if they have any Übelacker. The only things you might be in danger of coming across after doing that are the men in white coats.

As well as being a discerning collector, David is now a very active dealer and is currently enjoying himself travelling to auctions and fairs all over the world. I never knew him in his early collecting days, but it is hard to imagine him being any keener back then than he is today.

In many ways, looking for tin toys or very early trains can require a quite different collecting philosophy from that needed to seek out later trains and especially diecast toys, where people can collect in a more or less pre-defined series. Knowing what to look for has its attractions, and there is something comforting and controlling about being able to study the books and set your own collecting parameters. That possibly helps to explain why collecting diecast models and trains appeals to many more people, especially in Britain, than tin toys.

One very well known Swiss collector was the late Count Antonio Giansanti Coluzzi. On one occasion, my friend Trevor Goodman, when on a visit to see his daughter at school in Switzerland, had met with the Count at his apartment in Lausanne. At the time, which must have been around 1987, the Count had decided to sell his collection, although the auction which would take place at Christie's only a year or two later had still to be arranged. Trevor was becoming interested in gauge 1 trains, and after returning to England, had decided to buy a locomotive offered to him by the Count. I had neither met the renowned Swiss collector nor seen his collection, so when Trevor asked if I would like to join him in going over to collect his purchase, I was more than pleased and we arranged to spend a few days together in Switzerland.

The Count's collection was impressive. Everything was on show in display cases exactly as portrayed in his book 'The Trains on Avenue de Rumine'. Furthermore, the good news was that every single item could be bought. It was just like wandering through a huge top quality dealer's gallery. The only downside was that everything appeared so prohibitively expensive. I was looking at so many trains, asking the Count for various prices and desperately wanting to buy something, but finding it impossible.

I considered his Hornby 0 gauge collection, for which he quoted me a price, I recall, equating to about £9,000. I didn't buy it, although having later thought more deeply about some of the rarities, especially the French items, I wished I had. A dealer I knew from Paris in fact purchased the Hornby shortly afterwards. My single expenditure on the Count's trains was £400 for a pair of Bassett-Lowke 1921 series lithographed Southern Railway coaches.

Whether the Count, especially from my friendship with Trevor, had me earmarked as a big spender I am not sure, but if so, he concealed his disappointment remarkably well. The three of us spent a pleasant day together and I very much enjoyed looking over his fine collection of toy cars. The Count joined us at our hotel for dinner that evening, parking his maroon Rolls-Royce outside the front entrance. I put it that way, because most of us of course could never call such a vehicle simply a 'car'; it would always have to be referred to as a 'Rolls-Royce'.

A former stallholder of ours, Roy, a very nice man, used his Rolls-Royce for driving to the fairs every single time without fail. I can recall on at least two or three occasions overhearing someone at a fair, and always a person who must have been witness to Roy driving there dozens of times, say "Hello Roy! Have you come in your Rolls-Royce?" – I have to say, that never once did anyone take that sort of interest in my Ford Anglia.

It was through the Count that we were invited to visit Dr. Bommer and see his vast collection near Zurich. This indeed was a treat. We spent almost a full day there and looked at so many nice things. En route, we called to see the late Peter Ottenheimer in his shop also in Zurich. A very pleasant man with a shop full of great toys.

COLLECTING

19

My personal favourites

My collection is quite a small one. There are, however, just a few things which I particularly like. It is a bit of a mixed bag, but they all appeal for different reasons.

I have been a fan of Hornby 0 gauge trains ever since I first saw them running around. The No.2 Special tender locomotives – the LMS Compound, 'Yorkshire', 'Bramham Moor' and 'County of Bedford' – have always been my favourites; they just feel so exactly right in your hand. They are for me the perfect combination of a good model and a toy and as such they cannot be bettered. All versions of these locomotives are nice, but the earliest ones introduced in 1929 have a lovely rich subtlety of colour that I feel gives them the edge.

For a long while I had a bit of a fetish (what else can you call it?) for the Hornby Milk Tanker Wagons. It is the overscale bulbous appearance of the 'Nestlé's' and 'United Dairies' Tankers that appeals. Just like the Hornby No.2 Special locomotives, it is that same perfect blend of toy and model, coupled of course with real quality. I think I had as many as thirty boxed examples at one time, although that number is now pruned somewhat. In fact they are the only Hornby wagons I

Hornby late 1920s LMS Compound

Hornby 1930s LNER 'Yorkshire'

have ever seriously collected. It has always made more sense to me, if something has struck the right note, to collect multiples rather than try to get one of everything in the range. When it comes to collecting, we all have our quirks.

Bassett-Lowke has always been a byword for quality. My good friend and leading expert on the subject, Paul Aziz, has always considered the Märklin for Bassett-Lowke 'King George V' as his favourite in the range, which is easy to understand as it is a very attractive engine. Although my Bassett-Lowke 0 gauge locomotives are very few in number, I do have electric and clockwork examples of the King.

Hornby Nestlé's Milk Tank Wagon

Märklin for Bassett-Lowke 'King George V'

The Bassett-Lowke LMS and LNER streamlined locomotives have always had something of an aura about them. The LNER A4, when introduced in 1936 was priced at sixteen guineas (£16.80 in today's currency) This was a lot of money at the time and exactly four times the price of the company's own 'Flying Scotsman' in the catalogue at the comparatively bargain price of just four guineas. It can be no wonder, then, that so few A4s were sold.

A Bassett-Lowke Railways publication from 1969 suggests production figures of 200 for the LNER A4 and 300 for the Coronation class. This early estimate, which may have represented the intended production, is, however, way off the mark. There is no doubt that far fewer were actually made. Judging by the number I have seen and as a result of discussing the subject at length with friends, I would say it unlikely that in total any more than 25 to 30 of the LMS and the same number of the LNER models were actually built.

Watching the full size A4s racing down the main line as a boy has left me with fond memories of streamlined engines, which is why I have been so keen to obtain them

Bassett-Lowke A4 'Silver King'

Bassett-Lowke blue and maroon 'Coronation' class locomotives

in model form. It has been hard but pleasant work finding them. I imagine that the Bassett-Lowke A4 and Coronation class locomotives I have are the only group of four original ones together, one in each available colour. The A4 in silver grey is 'Silver King' and the blue A4 'Sir Nigel Gresley'. In LMS, the blue locomotive is 'Coronation' and in maroon 'Duchess of Gloucester'.

Whilst the Bassett-Lowke A4s were offered with a choice of alternative names, the LMS Coronation locomotives were officially produced with only the two mentioned above, although I have seen one genuine exception. In the early 1980s I went to look over a collection of trains belonging to a very pleasant man in Doncaster, who at one time maintained the real 'Flying Scotsman' when it belonged to Alan Pegler. As well as being knowledgeable on both real and model trains, he was also very accomplished at playing the organ, which he did whilst I was casting

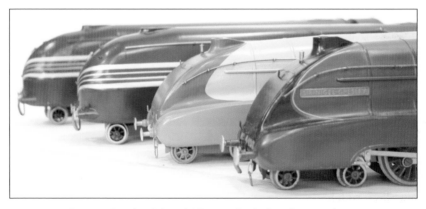

Bassett-Lowke A4 and 'Coronation' class locomotives

an eye over his collection. Perhaps there was something subtle in the music, like they have in supermarkets, to make you spend more, as I ended up buying everything he had.

His best item was a maroon streamlined Bassett-Lowke 'Duchess of Devonshire' and although the body had a keyhole, the mechanism inside was electric. He had acquired the locomotive many years earlier from Harold Elliott, a man well known for exhibiting his Bassett-Lowke layout both before and after the war. Mr. Elliott was a good friend of Mr. Bassett-Lowke and had received the locomotive from him personally. Although it began life in clockwork, Mr. Bassett-Lowke had arranged for an electric mechanism to be fitted so that Mr. Elliott could run the engine on his railway. Many years had passed since I had sold the 'Duchess' and it was nice to see it show up in a Rugby auction only four or five years ago, by that time fitted with a clockwork mechanism to match the body.

I did once see Harold Elliott's layout for myself when it was running in Scarborough, but as I can only have been about six or seven at the time, my memory

Harold Elliott with his layout in the 1950s – the 'Duchess of Devonshire' locomotive
is just visible to the right of centre

Bing for Bassett-Lowke gauge 1 'George The Fifth'

of it is vague. The one thing I do recall is the long express trains being brought to a halt, everything going quiet and then someone putting on what I can only think must have been a blue 'Percy' rather than a 'Thomas the Tank' engine to race round and round the track. This must have been done at intervals to amuse the kids and it sure did the trick with me.

When it comes to a toy train capturing the look and feel of the real thing, for my money the Bing for Bassett-Lowke range of locomotives take some beating, especially in gauge 1. When you consider that some of these were made in the years before the First World War, never mind the Second, the accuracy of their design and quality of construction is remarkable. Locomotives like the 'George The Fifth' and 'Sir Gilbert Claughton' have so much presence, especially in the larger gauge.

Far more collectors are interested in 0 gauge than anything bigger and, considering the scarcity of gauge 1, so much of it can still be bought relatively cheaply. Admittedly, special items like the Wainwright South East and Chatham 4-4-0 locomotive and tender or the Great Northern Stirling Single might set you back a

Bing for Bassett-Lowke gauge 1 SECR Wainwright class

pretty penny, but most gauge 1 models in the Bing for Bassett-Lowke range are no more expensive, and sometimes less so, than their smaller counterparts.

One locomotive I have could lay claim to something of a novel history. It was a personal favourite of none other than Mr. Bassett-Lowke himself and took pride of place perched on top of his office desk in Northampton. It is not, as you might expect, one of his company's top quality offerings, or even a special commission he was proud of. On the contrary, it is a crude little steam engine commonly known as a 'dribbler' and something not even made by his famous company. It was, as the man himself liked to put it "What trains were like before Bassett-Lowke started making them."

Whenever he had a talk to give on trains, Mr. Bassett-Lowke would take the engine along and delight in comparing this basic little steamer to the superb scale models his company was producing. On more than one occasion he can be seen photographed with it and an assortment of his fancy locomotives in 'The Bassett-Lowke Story' by Roland Fuller. The same little engine is also pictured near to the front of most editions of the Bassett-Lowke Model Railway Handbook. It looks exactly the same now, mark for mark, as it does in all the old photographs.

W.J. Bassett-Lowke with his little steam engine

Mr. Bassett-Lowke's little steam engine today

I am not a serious collector of hand-made models, although I do have one I am fond of. It is a one-inch to the foot model of a late 1920s Humber Touring Car made around that time by Ernest Twining, who for a long while worked in close co-operation with the Bassett-Lowke Company. The car is very similar in construction

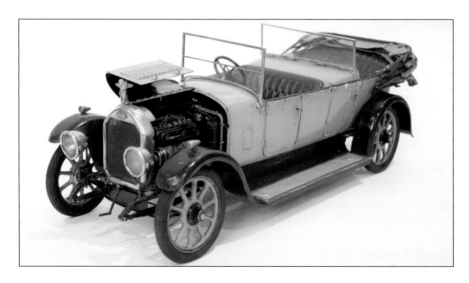

1920s Humber touring car by E.W. Twining

Engine detail in the Humber car

to the only others I know of by him, which were commissioned in the 1920s for Queen Mary's Dolls' House in Windsor Castle. The detail on the car is remarkable, particularly under the bonnet where the engine parts and even items like the hand tools are superbly modelled.

On the tin toy side, I was at one time very keen on 1920s and 1930s tin cars and had a good number of German examples and some of the French 1920s Citroën models. I still have a few, although I am not looking out for them especially any more. Japanese models of American cars I also had a fancy for at one time. I no longer collect these, although I am keen on Japanese models of British car marques like Triumph, Jaguar, MG and Rolls-Royce.

Perhaps what appeals to me above all else in collecting both trains and toys is lithographed or printed tinplate. Many of the early hand painted toys by companies like Märklin, Bing and others are of course wonderful. They are among the most sought after of toys and are all eagerly collected, but they are not for me. A printed tinplate vehicle carrying a company name or an advertisement for some product, as far as I am concerned, has more appeal.

Early English lithographed tin toys are the ones I am keenest on. Burnett, Chad Valley, Wells and Brimtoy are the main makers. Some of the early Burnett items, such as the First World War London Bus with all the advertisements I especially

1920s Citroën car

like. Their boxes are often nicely patriotic with an illustration of the vehicle shown against a Union Jack background. The tin printing on many of these early English vehicles is very appealing, particularly on delivery vans or tankers for companies like 'Lyons' or 'Shell' petrol.

One nice feature of collecting anything tin printed, I always think, is that it cannot really be faked or the condition 'improved'. Unlike anything with a painted finish, whatever state the lithographed item has survived in, it has to stand and be judged on its own two feet, or even four wheels, for all to see. On the train side, some of the Carette for Bassett-Lowke wagons in gauge 1 are fine examples of tin printing. The yellow 'Colman's Mustard', the 'Colman's Starch' and the yellow 'Bassett-Lowke' private owner van in particular, I like very much.

Two English 'Lyons' delivery vehicles

Burnett double decker bus

Carette for Bassett-Lowke 'Colman's Mustard' vans in both 1 and 0 gauges

Burnett 1920s Express Parcels van

Burnett 1930s Express Delivery van

Wells Shell-BP tanker

Burnett Rapid Omnibus

Burnett Royal Mail van

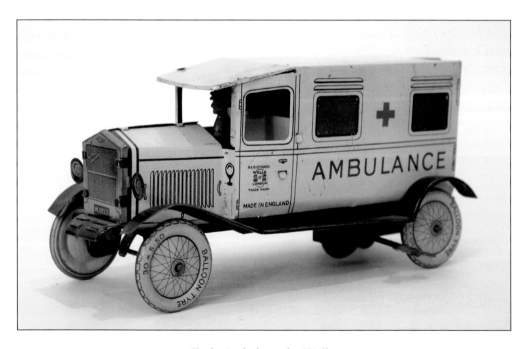

Early Ambulance by Wells

Chad Valley Royal Mail, Games van and CWS Crumpsall van

The Dennis delivery van advertising Chad Valley's range of board games is very well known. This and a Royal Mail van were made from identical pressings in the immediate post-war period. They must have been made for Chad Valley by another company, probably Metal Box, however, as a much earlier vehicle from the same pressings was produced in pre-war days, advertising 'CWS Crumpsall Cream Crackers'.

I once had another van made from this tooling, albeit in poor condition, in a brown livery advertising 'Meredith & Drew Biscuit Manufacturers'. I know this toy was based on a real vehicle, as a train collector friend of mine, examining my 'CWS Crumpsall' van among a display of toys I was showing at the Rugby Vintage Fair, told me that he used to drive an identical Dennis van, but for Meredith & Drew. This is one item that I would dearly like to get hold of to go with the others, but that really is the fun of it all. Knowing that a decent example is probably around somewhere or other gives you something to look out for. I dare say that for this particular item I would definitely be 'the right man'.

For a long time, I have been keen on tinplate biscuit tins in the shape of toys, especially vehicles. My original collection I sold in 1989, before starting again

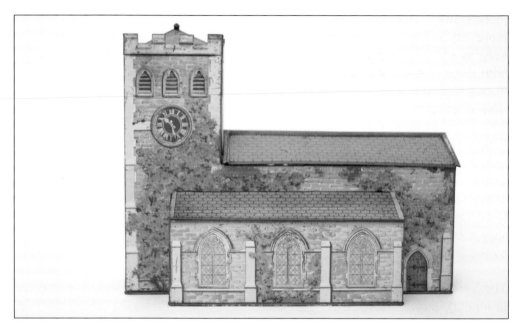

Victory 'V' church tin

Victory 'V' limousine

more slowly. The reason I say 'more slowly' is partly due to these things being more expensive today, but more down to the fact that I am now interested in keeping only a few pieces that I really like, rather than wanting to fill the house with them. I had about forty items in the first collection. In a few cases I have managed to find similar examples and occasionally in better condition than first time around.

When it comes to tins, all the Victory 'V' ones such as the limousine, or others modelled as such diverse subjects as churches, railway locomotives or children's cradles are huge and much bigger than most other branded novelty biscuit or sweet containers. I can only imagine that, unlike other companies' tins which were sold to customers as a complete filled package, these Victory ones must have stood on shop counters as a promotion for the lozenge company, and their contents dispensed by the shopkeeper, like would be done from a sweet jar.

The Victory limousine is a very imposing tin, not only for its large size (18 inches in length), but also for the delightful figures in the windows, especially the little girl holding her packet of Victory lozenges. The green limousine I have now is a fairly recent acquisition and although I was very pleased to get it, the price paid was higher than I care to remember (it is rarely much fun to remember those times when we have had to dig deep). The first one of these vehicles I came across and had in my earlier collection was almost identical to the one I have now, and in common with most good buys, the memory of getting it is a far more agreeable one to look back on.

It is a bit like anyone who likes a bet on the horses. They will always tell you about the good days – the ones when they had the winners – never the bad days. And after all who can blame them? We all like to remember the good times.

It was about 1980 when I heard about a large tin coming up in a house clearance auction in Leicester. This Victory limousine was an item I had never seen before and it was one of those occasions when the price it might make did not really come into the equation – I was determined to take it away no matter what. Other than two or three local dealers in antiques, I didn't recognise anyone in the saleroom, which even back then was a little unusual. I was stood there trying my best to play it cool and indifferent, like I couldn't care less (I must have learnt at least something from John Haley) and all the time thinking of how many hundreds it was going to cost me. When the hammer came down at £65, to say I was pleased would be a very mild way of putting it. Wouldn't it be nice if all buys in auction rooms could be like that? Only if you were the one doing the bidding of course.

As I was collecting the tin, I remember one of the dealers commenting on how he was not really surprised that it had made so much money as he thought it an interesting piece. It occurred to me that someone with those opinions, and that concept of value, was exactly the sort of person I wanted phoning me with toys to sell. I gave him my number, but never had a call.

My Macfarlane Lang 'Silver Link' tin has the original box and is the only novelty tin I have come across from pre-war days still having the biscuits inside, all wrapped in sturdy white paper into a neat rectangle and secured with a raffia type of string.

The only other toy I have with its edible contents still present is a 1950s Wells van made for Walter's Palm Toffee, again with its original box. I bought it from a friend of mine, Tony Dyche, at Sandown Park ten or fifteen years ago. All the 1950s toffees were still inside the van, except for one. Tony confessed that his young son had eaten it that morning on the way down to the fair – and I am pleased to report that he was still with us at the end of the day. It must be true what they say about the old days – things were definitely made to last.

Walters' Palm Toffee van

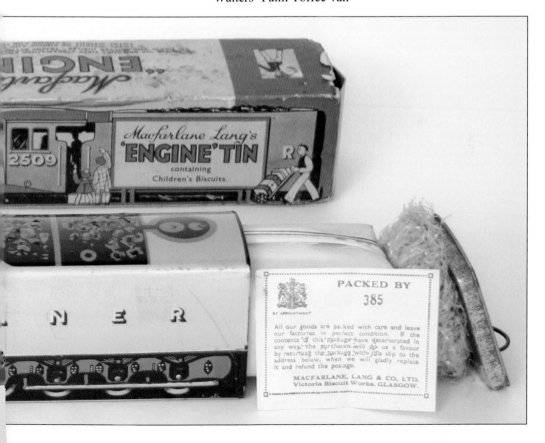

This then is the end of the book, but not the end of a journey that has been so much fun for so long on a train that I hope is not stopping, because I sure don't want to get off.

Something else I didn't want to get off